Case Studies in Human Services Consultation

A. Michael Dougherty

Western Carolina University

D1306944

Brooks/Cole Publishing Company

I(T)P *An International Thomson Publishing Company*

Pacific Grove • Albany • Bonn • Boston • Cincinnati • Detroit
London • Madrid • Melbourne • Mexico City • New York • Paris
San Francisco • Singapore • Tokyo • Toronto • Washington

• TO MY FAMILY •

A CLAIREMONT BOOK

Sponsoring Editor: Claire Verduin
Editorial Assistant: Gay C. Bond
Production Coordinator: Dorothy Bell
Cover Design: Roy R. Neuhaus

Printing and Binding: Malloy Lithographing, Inc.
COPYRIGHT © 1995 by Brooks/Cole Publishing Company
A Division of International Thomson Publishing Inc.
I(T)P The ITP logo is a trademark under license.

For more information, contact:

BROOKS/COLE PUBLISHING CO.
511 Forest Lodge Rd.
Pacific Grove, CA 93950
USA

International Thomson Editores
Campos Eliseos 385, Piso 7
Col. Polanco
11560 México D. F. México

International Thomson Publishing
Berkshire House 168-173
High Holborn
London WC1V 7AA
England

International Thomson Publishing Gmbh
Königwinterer Strasse 418
53227 Bonn
Germany

Thomas Nelson Australia
102 Dodds Street
South Melbourne, 3205
Victoria, Australia

International Thomson Publishing Asia
221 Henderson Road
#05-10 Henderson Building
Singapore 0315

Nelson Canada
1120 Birchmount Road
Scarborough, Ontario
Canada M1K 5G4

International Thomson Publishing–Japan
Hirakawacho Kyowa Building, 3F
2-2-1 Hirakawacho
Chiyoda-ku, 102 Tokyo
Japan

Printed in the United States of America

10 9 8 7 6 5 4 3 2 1

ISBN 0-534-25130-7

PREFACE

Case Studies in Human Services Consultation is the result of my increasing concern that in order to be effective as human services consultants, students need to have a sense of what goes on between a consultant and consultee during the consultation relationship. My discussions over the years with other professors who teach courses in consultation have led me to conclude that the most difficult aspect of teaching a consultation course is to "bring it alive"; that is, to help the student better see the links between theory and practice. To this end, in my course I typically have students go out and conduct a real-life consultation experience, make extensive use of role play, provide some instructional videos of consultations I have conducted, and discuss case studies provided in the text. Detailed case studies, such as those included in this text, can provide an added dimension in the attempt to help students not only understand what consultation is but also learn how to do it effectively. What I have tried to do is to present through these cases a cross-section of real-life human services consultation as it exists today.

Why use case studies as well as practice cases to assist students in becoming effective consultants? First, cases allow for some of the complex variables impacting the consultation process (such as its organizational context) to be analyzed and related to effective practice.

Second, cases bring novice consultants closer to real-life consultation. Third, cases provide specific situations which call for analysis and specific application. Hopefully, the habit of analyzing consultation situations is developed and will generalize to the consultant's real-life practice. Fourth, the cases reflect my view that the organizational context in which consultation occurs strongly influences the consultation process. For example, how a consultant would go about process consultation in a health care setting will vary from how process consultation is performed in a university counseling center. The cases used in this text represent a variety of settings, and will hopefully help the novice consultant gain insight into organizational dynamics as they affect the consultation process. Finally, cases make the reader an active participant. By being involved intellectually and emotionally with a case, the reader will most likely benefit more than from hearing a lecture about some aspect of consultation.

The structure of this book allows the reader to first obtain from Chapter One a brief overview of human services consultation. The reader then proceeds to read and analyze a case study in human services consultation in each of the next eight chapters. Each of the case study chapters is written according to the following prescribed format: setting and background issues; consultation goals; consultant function and role; consultee experience in consultation; consultant techniques and procedures employed through the stages of entry, diagnosis, implementation and disengagement; and references and suggested readings. Such a format should facilitate the identification across the cases of the major concepts and procedural dilemmas common to consultation practice. In Chapter Two, Larry Golden describes the Parent Consultation Center and the behaviorally-oriented brief family consultation approach it takes with its cases. Jon Carlson, in Chapter Three, writes about Adlerian parent consultation. In Chapter Four, Mary Deck and Glenda Isenhour discuss an innovative education/training consultation with school personnel. Pamela Carrington Rotto, in Chapter Five, relates a case of behavioral case consultation involving a teacher. In Chapter Six, Frances E. Tack and A. Michael Dougherty describe a case of process consultation with a university counseling center. In Chapter Seven, Liz Becker-Reems discusses a case of process consultation in a health care setting. Dick James, Walter Crews and Burl Gilliland in Chapter Eight relate an example of program consultation with a police department. In Chapter Nine, Frances E.

Tack and Lynn Hayes describe a fictitious mental health consultation case revolving around a client with AIDS. In Chapter Ten, I discuss the conclusions of these cases for the effective practice of human services consultation. I suggest in Chapter Eleven eight more cases for practice. These cases are open ended and each contains extenuating circumstances that make it challenging for the reader to determine how to proceed with the case.

Case Studies in Human Services Consultation is intended as a supplement to *Consultation: Practice and Perspectives in School and Community Settings* (Second Edition, 1995) or any other basic text in human services consultation. I make the assumption in *Case Studies in Human Services Consultation* that the reader is in the process of being familiarized, or already familiarized, with the literature on human services consultation. This text can be used alone with advanced students in seminars, practicum and internship courses.

ACKNOWLEDGMENTS

I would like to thank Dr. Larry Golden of the University of Texas at San Antonio for his ideas on getting a text such as this off the ground. Thanks to my graduate assistant Nancy Gore for helping me get all of the manuscripts into the correct word processing programs and for typing some of the manuscript. I offer special thanks to my secretary Judy Revere for her encouragement, keeping me organized, and helping with the manuscript in a variety of ways. I am grateful to all of the contributors for taking time from their busy schedules and helping produce a quality text. I am indebted to my family for all of the love and support they provided me during the term of this project. Finally, to the fine people at Brooks/Cole, a big thank you for all of the support and professional assistance in allowing this project to come to fruition.

CONTENTS

CHAPTER THREE

CHAPTER FOUR

CHAPTER FIVE

CHAPTER SIX

CHAPTER SEVEN

CHAPTER EIGHT

CHAPTER ONE

INTRODUCTION

A. Michael Dougherty

Overview of This Book

One of the most difficult things to learn in any of the helping
relationships is getting down to the "nitty-gritty" and actually
helping someone. This is certainly true of human services
consultation. It is one thing to know theories and concepts related
to consultation and another to be able to apply them effectively.
One way to attempt to link theories and concepts with effective
practice is studying actual consultation cases. Case studies can
help answer the question: "What do experienced and effective
consultants 'know' about consultation when they consult?" One
thing they know is the practical wisdom about the common
circumstances encountered in their work. Case studies allow
prospective consultants to tap that practical wisdom. Another
thing that experienced and effective consultants most likely know
is that they carry their own "personal baggage" to the consultation
process. By reading the cases of experienced consultants, perhaps
prospective consultants will become more aware of some of their
own personal issues and better understand how these issues may
impact their consultation practice.

1

The main purposes of this text are to provide you, through exposure to consultation cases, with a view of real-life consultation and assist you in beginning to develop your own personalized style of consultation. By reading how practicing consultants actually consult, you can obtain a better grasp of the nuts and bolts of real-life consultation. By being asked to analyze and discuss these cases, you will hopefully be able to identify a sense of "who you are" as a consultant and thus begin to forge a personalized approach to consultation.

In this first chapter, I present an overview of human services consultation. In each of the following eight chapters (Chapters Two-Nine), one or more practicing consultants present a consultation case. Each case shows how a certain approach to consultation is applied in a given setting. At the end of each case, you are asked to critically analyze that case, choose five things you would do differently, and justify your choices.

Following the case study chapters, I attempt to pull together the ideas of the case contributors in a chapter dedicated to implications for effective practice. In Chapter Eleven, I provide eight additional practice cases for your consideration. For each case in Chapter Eleven there is a brief description of the case itself along with some limitations I have chosen to put on that case. You are then asked to use that information to determine how you would proceed as the consultant in the case.

It is important to review the basics of human services consultation to provide a common ground for exploring the cases. The next section of this chapter provides you with a brief overview of human services consultation. First, I define consultation and list its characteristics. Next, I note the skills consultants need to be effective and the roles they frequently take on. Finally, I briefly discuss ethical behavior in consultation and some popular models.

Human Services Consultation

Consultation is practiced by human service professionals such as counselors, psychologists and social workers in a variety of settings. For example, a counselor educator assists the staff of a counseling center in identifying its major work concerns and in making plans to solve them.

When human services professionals consult, their primary purpose is to help their consultees to work more effectively with the concerns that led to the request for consultation. Clearly, consultation is a helping relationship. Consultation can be defined as *a process in which a human service professional assists a consultee with a work-related (or caretaking-related) problem with a client system, with the goal of helping both the consultee and the client system in some specified way* (Dougherty, 1995). Human service consultants usually consult with other professionals as well as parents of children. The client system can consist of an individual, group, organization, or the entire community.

Characteristics of Consultation

Consultation has many agreed-upon characteristics. Here is a list of some of the more common characteristics of consultation:

* Consultation is a problem-solving process.
* Consultation is triadic in nature; the three parties being the consultant, the consultee and the client system. The consultant delivers direct service to the consultee who delivers direct service to the client system. The consultant provides indirect service to the client system by providing direct service to the consultee.
* The goal of consultation is to help both the consultee and the client system in some way.

3

* The consultant can be either internal or external to the system in which consultation is to occur.
* Participation in consultation is totally voluntary for all of the parties involved.
* The relationship between the consultant and consultee is one of peers and tends to be collaborative whenever possible.
* The consultation relationship is a temporary one.
* Consultation deals exclusively with work-related (or caretaking-related) problems. The personal problems of the consultee are not dealt with.

Skills Necessary for Effective Consultation

To be effective, consultants need to have a personal and professional growth orientation, knowledge of consultation and human behavior, and skills in consulting. Many skills are required to be effective as a consultant. The importance of **communication and interpersonal skills** is increasingly being pointed out. Competence in **problem-solving skills** is essential as consultation is problem-solving by its very nature. **Skills in working with organizations** are increasingly important as more human service consultants are engaging in organizational consultation. Because consultants are increasingly being called upon to work with groups of consultees, **skills in group work** are important for consultants to possess. Because we live in a culturally diverse society, **skills in dealing with cultural diversity** are essential so that the consultants can discern the complex role diversity takes on in their work. In order to be effective, consultants need skills which allow them to behave **ethically and professionally**.

Common Consultant Roles

Consultants can take on a variety of roles in any given consultation relationship. The primary role a consultant takes on depends on a variety of factors such as the consultant's abilities, values and frame of reference; the consultee's expectations and skill level; the nature of the consultation problem; and the environmental context in which consultation is occurring.

Consultant roles are often described as running on a continuum from directive to nondirective (Lippitt & Lippitt, 1986). The following are six common roles taken on by consultants:

*   **Advocacy**: This most directive of consultant roles has the consultant persuading a consultee to take some course of action.
*   **Expert**: This is the most common role consultants take on and consists of the consultant providing the consultee with some knowledge, advice or service.
*   **Trainer/Educator**: In this role, the consultant facilitates skill and/or knowledge acquisition in the consultee.
*   **Collaborator:** In human services consultation, consultants frequently attempt to involve consultees as joint problem solvers in all steps of the consultation process with the exception of the implementation phase.
*   **Fact Finder:** In this role, the consultant typically gathers information, analyzes it, and feeds it back to the consultee.
*   **Process Specialist:** In this least directive role, the consultant focuses on the process events; that is, on *how* things are being done instead of on *what* is being done.

Ethical Behavior

Throughout their careers all consultants encounter ethical dilemmas about which they must make decisions. What kinds of ethical dilemmas might you face as a consultant? The list provides many of the areas in which ethical dilemmas can arise due to the various issues they generate for practicing consultants:

* The influence of one's values
* Consultant competence
* Training consultants
* The complexity of the consultant-consultee-client system relationship
* The rights of consultees
* Selection of interventions
* Working with groups

Professional codes of ethics can provide only general guidelines for ethical practice. The bottom line is that consultants, within these broad guidelines, need to make informed, sound and responsible judgments based on ethical decision making.

A Generic Model of Consultation

Whatever skills consultants use, whatever roles they take on, whatever ethical dilemmas they encounter, they typically have a model of consultation that guides their practice. I present here an overview of a generic model of consultation (Dougherty, 1995) to help you develop a framework for analyzing the cases which follow in the later chapters of this text. All consultation involves relationship building, definition of a problem, implementation and evaluation of a plan, and disengagement. I have chosen four stages each with four corresponding phases to make up the generic model. As you will note in the cases you read, no real life consultation experience will parallel each and every stage and phase of this model. In real life consultation, the stages of the generic model will overlap. For example, it is common that when a new aspect of the problem arises, the consultation process reverts back to the problem definition stage. There is nothing magic about having four stages each with four phases to make up this generic model of consultation. They simply are the results of how I view the consultation process. I have tried to put together a model which describes the consultation process in general enough terms to include most of the cases you will be reading later on in this text.

Stage One - **entry** - consists of the phases of exploring organizational needs, contracting, physically entering the system, and psychologically entering the system. During the entry stage, the consultant attempts to get a general feel for the problem(s) to be dealt with in the consultation relationship, develops some form of working agreement with the parties involved, sets up a physical presence within the organization, and starts building relationships with those involved in consultation. A key point about entry is that the consultant must "enter" with each consultee with whom they come into contact.

Stage Two - **diagnosis** - involves the phases of gathering information, defining the problem, setting goals, and generating possible interventions. The consultant and/or consultee can gather data to shed further light on the problem through use of observations, surveys and questionnaires, examining records, and interviewing. The consultant and consultee define the problem by analyzing and interpreting the information that has been gathered. They then set goals to solve or cope with the defined problem. The diagnosis stage concludes with the consultant and consultee generating a series of possible interventions, some of which can be put into a plan for resolving the problem.

Stage Three - **implementation** - consists of the phases of choosing an intervention, formulating a plan, implementing the plan, and evaluating the plan. The stage begins with the consultant and consultee selecting activities they believe have a strong chance of positively affecting the problem. With these interventions in mind, the consultant and consultee carefully develop a plan that is tailored to the unique aspects of the problem. The consultee then implements that plan with the consultant being "on call" for the purpose of providing any needed assistance. After the plan has been implemented, it is evaluated. Based on the results of the evaluation, the consultation process either moves to developing another plan or on to the disengagement stage.

Stage Four - **disengagement** - consists of the phases of evaluating the consultation process, planning postconsultation matters, reducing involvement and following up, and terminating. This stage is the "winding down" of the consultation relationship. Evaluation of the consultation process is a planned event and can be accomplished in a variety of ways ranging from a face-to-face meeting with the consultee to the use of consultee satisfaction surveys. Postconsultation planning involves determining how the consultee is going to take care of the "business" of maintaining the effects of consultation. The consultant then reduces involvement by becoming increasingly less active in dealing with the situation for which consultation was sought. The consultant, however, engages in agreed-upon follow up activities. Terminating is the formal ending of the consultation process.

A final note on the generic model: consultation is a helping relationship. It needs to be conducted with a personal touch. I am of the opinion that, to be effective, the generic model should be implemented by a consultant who recognizes this.

Models of Consultation

There are three theoretical models of consultation that are very popular. These models include organizational, mental health, and behavioral consultation. The name associated with a given model serves to identify that model's given focus. *Organizational consultation* tends to consider the entire organization to be the client system; that is, the goal is to enhance the overall effectiveness of the organization in some way. *Mental health consultation* focuses on the mental health implications for organizations and consultees' clients; that is, it attempts to ameliorate the psychological well being of the parties involved. *Behavioral consultation* typically focuses on specific changes in the client, client system and/or consultee. You will want to remember that these models are more alike than different. They vary more in what they emphasize than in their nature. All of these models can be practiced in a variety of settings ranging from business and industry to schools.

Organizational consultation. Organizational consultation tends to define the problem in terms of an organization's structure or processes. For example, a consultant may help an organization reorganize (i. e., change structure) or help members changes the way they communicate (i. e., change processes). The goal of organizational consultation is to help alleviate a problem through carefully designed interventions that affect the organization's system. There is no one set model of organizational consultation, but rather a series of approaches. The most popular approaches are the purchase of expertise model, the doctor/patient model and the process model (Schein, 1988).

When consultees request help from consultants, they frequently seek some form of **expertise**. Expertise can take the form of knowledge and/or skill. Some combination of information, methods, tools and support is provided to the consultee. This model by its nature is very content oriented. The purchase of expertise model is most appropriate when the problem has been well defined, such as when a consultant provides specific information or training or when a glitch arises in a human service program. Two common forms of the purchase of expertise model

9

are the *education/training consultation* and *program consultation*. Consultants provide education training consultation in a variety of settings, often in the form of workshops. In this text, you will read a unique case of education/training consultation written by Mary Deck and Glenda Eisenhower. In program consultation, the organization uses a consultant in some way such as assisting in planning a new program, revising an existing program, or dealing with factors that affect a current program. In this text Dick James, Walter Crews and Burl Gilliland provide a relatively complex case that describes program consultation.

In the **doctor/patient** model, a consultant is called in because the organization knows something is wrong but doesn't know what that "something" is. The consultant is given the power to make a diagnosis and prescribe a solution. For example, a consultant from a community counseling center is hired to assist a university counseling center in becoming more effective in delivering services by examining the center and making a series of recommendations based on that examination.

In **process consultation**, the consultant typically works with a small group of consultees for the purpose of focusing on their interactions. The interactions of the consultees, such as the way they hold meetings, are assumed to be the source of the problem. By helping consultees examine their own interactions and ways of doing things, process consultation attempts to create organizational change through changes in the ways consultees interact with one another. In this text, Tack and Dougherty present a form of process consultation that was used with the staff of a university counseling center. Becker-Reems describes a case in which process consultation was used in a hospital setting.

Mental health consultation. Mental health consultation is based on the idea that society's mental health can be promoted through the efforts of consultants who work with other human service professionals, teachers, parents, and other community members.

10

Mental health consultation was originally heavily influenced by psychodynamic theory (Caplan & Caplan, 1993). This type of consultation typically takes the form of either *case consultation* or *program consultation*. Consultees are considered to have problems with work-related or caregiving-related tasks due to one or more of the following reasons: lack of knowledge, lack of skill, lack of confidence, and/or lack of objectivity. A major goal of this model is to improve the consultee's ability to function in the future. In this text, Tack and Hayes present an example of mental health case consultation. In addition, Carlson presents an example of a parent group based on Adlerian psychology.

Behavioral consultation. Behavioral consultation is based on social learning theory and attempts to apply behavioral technology to resolve the problem being dealt with in consultation. Behavioral consultants typically aim for specific changes and employ specific goals in their work (Bergan & Kratochwill, 1990). In behavioral consultation, the consultant and consultee use a problem-solving sequence that first uses behavioral terminology to describe the problem. Next, a functional analysis of the problem examines what happened before and after the problem occurred. Once a target behavior has been chosen, behavioral objectives are defined in terms of desired changes and a behavior change program is designed to achieve those objectives. The program is then implemented and rigorously evaluated. Behavioral consultation typically takes on one of three forms: behavioral case consultation, behavioral system consultation, and behavioral technology training. In this text, Carrington-Rioto presents a case of behavioral consultation with a teacher. In addition, Golden presents a case of behaviorally-oriented parent consultation.

In **behavioral case consultation** a consultant provides direct, behavior-based service to a consultee concerning the management of a client or group of clients assigned to the consultee. In **behavioral system consultation**, behavioral technology principles are applied to a social system such as an organization. Behavioral system consultants use behavior technology principles to analyze and change interactions among the various subsystems of the larger social system. In **behavioral technology training**, consultants provide consultees with training to increase their general usage of behavioral technology when working with clients. The principles and methods of the education/training model discussed above apply to behavioral technology training.

Where We Are Going From Here

Having received an overview of consultation, we are now ready to consider some specific cases. As noted earlier, each of the next eight chapters presents you with a consultation case. As you read these chapters, think about what it must have been like to be a consultant involved with the case. At the end of each chapter you are asked to apply your own personal view of the case by determining how you might proceed differently from the authors. After the case chapters you are provided with a chapter that pulls together the main ideas in the cases and cites implications for effective practice. After that chapter, you are provided with a final chapter that lets you apply what you have learned to a series of practice cases.

References and Suggested Readings

Bergan, J. R., & Kratochwill, T. R. (1990). Behavioral consultation and therapy. New York: Plenum Press.
Caplan, G., & Caplan, R. B. (1993). Mental health consultation and collaboration. San Francisco, CA: Jossey-Bass.
Dougherty, A. M. (1995). Consultation: Practice and perspectives in school and community settings. (2nd ed.). Pacific Grove, CA: Brooks/Cole.

Lippitt, G., & Lippitt, R. (1986). <u>The consulting process in action</u>. (2nd ed.). La Jolla, CA: University Associates.

Schein, E. H. (1988). <u>Process consultation: Its role in organization development</u>. Volume I. Reading, MA: Addison-Wesley.

CHAPTER TWO

THE PARENT CONSULTATION CENTER:

A TIME-LIMITED BEHAVIORALLY-ORIENTED

APPROACH

Larry Golden

Setting and Background Issues

<u>Setting</u>. In 1987, I received a $5,000 award from the Counseling and Human Development Foundation (CHDF). The CHDF, a philanthropic agency of the American Counseling Association, provides seed money for innovative projects. While I've been associated with other "soft money" projects, this one has had the distinction of continuing after the grant money ran out! Founded in 1987, the Parent Consultation Center (PCC) is developing a history of continuous service.

The Parent Consultation Center is housed in an elementary school in Northside Independent School District in San Antonio, Texas. The school district incurs the obligation of keeping the school open during evening hours. Families can come to the PCC from throughout the district to receive free services. A short-term, behaviorally-oriented approach to consultation called brief family consultation is used at the PCC. This approach enlists the home and school in an attempt to ameliorate children's behavior problems.

Background. Sam, a fourth-grader, fails to complete classroom assignments. He is sullen and then disrespectful when confronted by his teacher, Ms. Jonas. She sends him to Mr. Smyth, the counselor. Mr. Smyth asks Sam to share his views about what's wrong. Sam says he doesn't have a clue. As this matter is discussed further, Sam shares the thought that he thinks Ms. Jonas hates him.

As the session continues Sam owns the fact that he is not doing his part in trying to learn in Ms. Jonas' class. Mr. Smyth suggests that together they look at some of the consequences of Sam's not completing his homework assignments. Sam notes that he will probably get another "bad" report card. "And what will happen at home if you bring home a bad report card?" asks Mr. Smyth.

"I don't think much will happen because I don't think my mom really cares about how I do in school," responds Sam. Nonetheless, Mr. Smyth encourages Sam to try his best in class and gets Sam to agree to a behavioral contract in which Sam agrees to immediately start finishing seventy percent of his assignments and work toward a one hundred percent completion rate. With the consent of his teacher, Sam will be given some free time on the computer in the school counseling suite as a reward as his homework assignment completion rate progressively increases. Mr. Smyth gets Sam's permission to follow up with his mother concerning the contract and invites Sam to come and talk whenever he would like. When Mr. Smyth follows up with a phone call to Sam's home, the mother says: "Do whatever you need to do to get him to do his work." Although Sam's problem is impacted by the home, the total responsibility for resolving it is effectively given away to the school.

The above vignette of counselor-to-student direct service is uncomfortably familiar. It can be very difficult for counselors to effectively help children at school when it is apparent that the child's home situation is significantly impacting the problem being dealt with at school and parent involvement is minimal. Counselors frequently attempt to do their best in trying to help children with school-related problems while neglecting to effectively involve the significant adults who are influencing the concerns the child is experiencing. It is frequently more efficient to consult with parents and teachers about a child's concerns as a supplement to or even a substitute for direct counseling services to children. Dealing with the family directly is important in that the family is in a powerful position to support or sabotage (as in Sam's case) the best efforts of a counselor to help its children.

I thought about how quality family involvement in ameliorating children's problems could be accomplished. With the exception of responding to emergencies, today's working parents are often not available during school hours. Further, most school counselors have neither the training nor administrative sanction to conduct family therapy. Consequently, I developed the idea of a Parent Consultation Center to help families after the work day and provide an alternative to referral to family therapy.

Consultation Goals

The goal of brief family consultation is simply stated: To resolve a child's behavior problems in five or less consultation sessions with the child and his or her parents.

When we opened the PCC's doors to the public, it was a big temptation to declare, "Send us your dysfunctional and chaotic!" But such a misguided goal would have exposed dysfunctional families as well as consultants to inevitable failure. It's bad enough that failure in a helping relationship is embarrassing to the parties involved. Even worse, a failed helping relationship sets up a "Nothing works!" attitude that makes it less likely that help will be sought by the family when needed in the future. Clearly, there had to be an understanding of the limits of our time-limited behavioral consultation model. Brief family consultation, like family therapy, is based on systems theory and focuses on the dynamics of the family system in the consultation sessions. I was confident that brief family consultation may be an excellent treatment choice for a misbehaving child in a functional family.

The dangers of being indiscriminate in consulting can be illustrated by a case from the early years of my own private practice. A fourth-grader, Frederick, was referred by school authorities because of violent outbursts. Frederick was a southern boy with good manners. I guess those "Yes, Sirs" and "No, Sirs" must have bedazzled me because I arranged a consultation session to include his parents and school authorities after the first interview. Disaster! I had failed to observe gross problems in this family that exploded in a violent confrontation between the parents in front of the teacher, counselor, and assistant principal. An embarrassing waste of time was had by all!

In planning the Parent Consultation Center, I decided that there would be no "walk-ins." Families would be referred by school counselors who would serve as gatekeepers. They would refer functional families to the PCC for brief family consultation and dysfunctional families to other community resources for family therapy. Of course, dysfunctional families could be mistakenly referred to the PCC and, in practice, sometimes are. When

17

consulting with dysfunctional families, the targeted behaviors are severely narrowed so there is a reasonable chance that the behaviors can be achieved and/or an appropriate referral arranged for the family.

How can one discriminate between functional and dysfunctional families? I recommend an assessment tool called the Quick Assessment of Family Functioning (Golden, 1988). There is some support for the instrument's predictive power (Golden, 1988). I will briefly describe the five variables that enable the referring counselor to discriminate between functional and dysfunctional families and thereby make an appropriate decision regarding whether or not to offer consultation.

1. Parental Resources. Can the parents provide for the child's basic needs and still have time and energy left over to follow through on a behavioral plan? A strong marriage, supportive extended family, gainful employment, and financial security are conditions that predict that a family can "hold up its end" in a team approach. On the other extreme, very young, immature single parents are likely to have fewer resources at their disposal. Issues such as multi-generational poverty, criminality, alcoholism, suicide threats, and child abuse are "survival" level problems far beyond the scope of brief family consultation.

2. Time Frame of Problem Behavior. Is the child's misbehavior of short or chronic duration? It stands to reason that a brief strategy will work better with short-term problems.

3. Communication. Can family members communicate well enough to solve problems? It's difficult to solve problems if family members are unable to talk about them effectively.

4. Hierarchy of Authority. Are parents effective in asserting authority? Parents in functional families hold an "executive" position in the family organization. Children are granted freedom commensurate with their demonstrated responsibility. In dysfunctional families, parents surrender authority, often in the hope that conflict with a child can be avoided. Children in such families are often out of control. Family therapy is recommended when the hierarchy of parental authority is disturbed.

5. Rapport Between Helping Adults. Can parents and helping professionals work together in a team effort to resolve a child's behavior problem? Parent dependability is a factor. Do these parents return phone calls? Are they punctual for conferences? Central to the issue is follow through; the functional family does its "homework." A breakdown can occur at the professional level, as well. For example, a "burned out" teacher may be more invested in documenting a disruptive child's "ticket" to a special education program than in assisting in a plan to improve the child's classroom behavior.

Quick Assessment of Family Functioning

Respond to questions on a scale of 1 to 5.

1 Definitely no   2 No   3 Moderately   4 Yes   5 Definitely yes

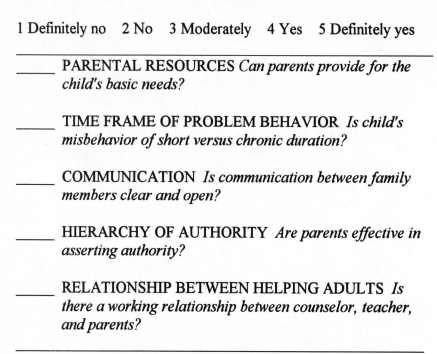

_____ PARENTAL RESOURCES *Can parents provide for the child's basic needs?*

_____ TIME FRAME OF PROBLEM BEHAVIOR *Is child's misbehavior of short versus chronic duration?*

_____ COMMUNICATION *Is communication between family members clear and open?*

_____ HIERARCHY OF AUTHORITY *Are parents effective in asserting authority?*

_____ RELATIONSHIP BETWEEN HELPING ADULTS *Is there a working relationship between counselor, teacher, and parents?*

<u>Limitations of Brief Family Consultation</u>. Brief family consultation is a behavioral approach that typically works well with elementary school children and less well with adolescents. Typically, young children trust that the adults in their lives know what is best for them and respond eagerly to rewards and praise. Adolescents, on the other hand, may regard adults as agents of control and resent the manipulation inherent in "carrot and stick" tactics. In fact, I am of the opinion that teenagers respond better to a cognitive-behavioral approach that is congruent with their developing need to become increasingly independent and autonomous.

Brief family consultation is a time-limited approach that is unlikely to have a significant impact on serious personal or systemic dysfunction. This is why the referral process should deselect children with severe personal problems and dysfunctional families.

Finally, brief family consultation depends on the participation of a child's significant others. In common with other systemic approaches, its impact is diminished when a key adult player fails to regularly attend or adequately "buy into" the consultation process.

Consultant Function and Role

Logistics. The Parent Consultation Center is administered by a school counselor who receives a small honorarium from the school district. Other school counselors volunteer their services. Counselors-in-training from local universities work at the center as part of their practicum/internship experiences. These students are teamed with professional counselors until the students are ready to conduct supervised consultation on their own. In brief family consultation, consultants contact referring school counselors after the first conference to inform them that the family has followed through. Parents are encouraged to phone their child's teacher to work out a plan for monitoring and reporting.

Procedures. The consultant meets with the parents and the child. Together, the parties involved write a behavior contract (see **TARGET BEHAVIOR FORM**). During this process, the consultant challenges the family to set goals that can be realistically achieved in a time frame taken up by the five consultation sessions.

21

TARGET BEHAVIOR FORM

Child _____   Conference # _____

1. _____

    This target behavior is being achieved now.
    (definitely not)   1   2   3   4   5   (definitely)

2. _____

    This target behavior is being achieved now.

3. _____

    This target behavior is being achieved now.
    (definitely not)   1   2   3   4   5   (definitely)

What will happen during the coming week?

What will parent do?
_____

What will child do?
_____

What will consultant do?

_____

Next conference date _____Time_____

_____

The consultant supports parental authority. Parents are treated with respect, even deference because it is likely that the misbehaving child is making a plea, albeit indirect, for increased parental control. Once they feel guilt and confusion, even competent parents may permit the child more freedom than is appropriate. The consultant encourages parents to take charge of resources that could serve as reinforcers. For example, a child who is "independently wealthy," sporting a big allowance and a room full of electronic games, is in a position to disregard his parents' demands for behavior change. These parents would be advised to take steps to terminate the allowance and remove the games. The parents would then be encouraged to allow the child to earn these items back as rewards for achieving behavioral goals set during consultation.

When appropriate, the consultant brings both parents together in a team effort. If marital conflict surfaces, the consultant pushes for unity on behalf of the child. This intervention by the consultant points to a distinction between a consultative and therapeutic model. In family *therapy*, marital conflict would be "worked through" with the assistance of a family counselor or therapist. In brief family consultation, the consultant tells parents they must agree on only three things if they are to help their child: (a) the target behaviors, (b) how progress will be monitored, and (c) consequences. Such an agreement is then sought and negotiated.

The team effort also frequently includes school personnel. All too often family therapists get fully involved with family dynamics but do not pay adequate attention to the role and impact of school personnel in ameliorating the problem. Clearly, consultants conducting brief family consultation need to involve school personnel in the consultation process when possible.

Consultee Experience in Consultation

Typically, parents first learn about the Parent Consultation Center from the school counselor who makes the referral. The counselor informs them that the PCC has evening hours, that there is no fee, and, most important, that they are good candidates to benefit from

23

an intervention that is limited to five conferences. The limit of five conferences spurs the consultees to an intensive "do or die" effort.

It is then up to the parents to schedule an appointment for themselves and their child. Arriving at the PCC at the appointed time, the family meets their consultant(s). Since the PCC operates in the evenings, the conferences can be held in school offices or classrooms, perhaps a more comfortable setting than a therapist's office. It is important for families to know that they will not receive "therapy." To make this distinction explicit, the face-to-face meetings are termed "conferences" not "sessions," and the practitioners call themselves "consultants" not "counselors."

Progress is reviewed during each conference and targets and consequences are fine-tuned and recorded on the target behavior form. The family takes a copy of this form home as a reminder to follow through on agreed-upon behaviors. The child typically receives an encouraging phone call or a postcard in the mail from the consultant during the week.

Parents usually come away from the first conference with an assignment to phone the classroom teacher and set up a plan for monitoring and reporting the child's behavior. No secret is made of this fact as the parties involved want children to know that the adults in their lives are cooperating for the child's welfare.

Finally, at the fifth and last interview, progress is assessed and gains celebrated. Plans are discussed for maintaining and building upon new behaviors. At the time of termination, if conditions dictate, an appropriate referral to family therapy is made.

Application: Consultant Techniques and Procedures

I am grateful to Victor Rangel, a school counselor, for contributing this case study from the Parent Consultant Center in San Antonio, Texas. Of course, every effort has been made to protect the confidentiality of the consultees.

Entry. During the "entry" stage the consultant (Victor) initiated a working relationship. The parameters of the problem were examined and a tentative contract developed and agreed upon.

The consultees in this case were ten-year-old Felix Seguro and his mother, Linda, and Mr. Raul Zapata, Felix' teacher. The presenting problems were that Felix had a tendency to talk back to his teacher and fight with peers. Felix lived with his mother, Linda; an older sister, Sylvia (18); and his stepfather, Henry. Felix had only occasional contact with his natural father who lived in a distant city.

The results of the "Quick Assessment of Family Functioning" indicated that Felix and his family were acceptable candidates for brief family consultation (see "Seguro Family -- Quick Assessment of Family Functioning"). Their very average score of 2.8 on the instrument was viewed by the consultant (Victor), however, with great enthusiasm. For Victor, the family's mere attendance at the conference demonstrated their commitment to change and provided hope that Felix, his family and the school will receive the benefits of a successful consultation.

Diagnosis. "Diagnosis" is an ongoing part of the consultative process involving problem formulation and goal setting. With a maximum of five conferences during this consultation relationship, the consultant knew that he had to formulate at least a tentative diagnosis at the first interview.

Seguro Family
Quick Assessment of Family Functioning

Respond to questions on a scale of 1 to 5.
1 Definitely no   2 No   3 Moderately   4 Yes   5 Definitely yes

---

4 PARENTAL RESOURCES *Can parents provide for the child's basic needs?*
Linda and Henry (stepfather) both work and provide a "good home" for Felix.

3 TIME FRAME OF PROBLEM BEHAVIOR *Is child's misbehavior of short versus chronic duration?*
The misbehavior started about two years ago, coincidental with the divorce.

2 COMMUNICATION *Is communication between family members clear and open?*
A discussion between Linda and Felix usually deteriorates into an argument.

2 HIERARCHY OF AUTHORITY *Are parents effective in asserting authority?*
Linda tolerates misbehavior rather than risk a confrontation.   Henry is not much help.

3 RELATIONSHIP BETWEEN HELPING ADULTS *Is there a working relationship between counselor, teacher, and parents?*
Linda distrusts Mr. Zapata and defends Felix when Mr. Zapata punishes him (sending him to the office). Linda has good rapport with Victor.

Goal 1. Felix will take charge of his own emotions and behaviors.
In classic "external versus internal locus of control" style, Felix placed responsibility for his misbehavior on others. For example, Felix declined all responsibility for disrupting the class, "Mr. Zapata puts my name on the board for not doing anything."

<u>Goal 2.</u> <u>Linda (the mother) will enforce consequences at home and</u> <u>stop shielding Felix from consequences at school</u>. Out of frustration and distrust of school authorities, Linda has been protecting Felix from the negative consequences he deserves.

<u>Goal 3.</u> <u>Mr. Zapata (the teacher) will participate in a working</u> <u>relationship between Linda and Felix</u>. Mr. Zapata had more or less given up on Felix and has tended to regard him as an incorrigible trouble maker. Mr. Zapata has responded to Linda's defenses and complaints on Felix' behalf by limiting his interventions to documentation and punishment of Felix' behavior.

In brief family consultation, goals and strategies are linked with the Target Behavior Form which is completed at each and every conference. While the targeted behaviors can be altered or even dropped, in Felix' case, they remained consistent throughout the five conferences: (1) stop fighting with other students, (2) be respectful to Mr. Zapata, (3) finish assigned school work.

<u>Implementation</u>. During the implementation stage, Victor pursued the crucial cognitive shift of getting Felix to understand that only he, Felix, could control his emotions. Blaming others would merely delay self-mastery. Some transcribed dialogue from a family consultation session with the family illustrates Victor's strategy.

Felix -- I did real good Wednesday until he (Mr. Zapata) made me get angry.

Victor -- I understand what you're saying, but let's try something here. Let me ask you a question: <u>Who</u> made you get angry?

Later in the conference, Victor pointedly asked, "Which is easier, to control what others do or control yourself?"

27

TARGET BEHAVIOR FORM

Child _Felix Seguro_   Conference # _1_

1.   _Stop fighting with other kids_
      This target behavior is being achieved now.
      (definitely not)   1   _2_   3   4   5   (definitely)

2.   _Be respectful to Mr. Zapata_
      This target behavior is being achieved now.
      (definitely not)   _1_   2   3   4   5   (definitely)

3.   _Finish my assigned work_
      This target behavior is being achieved now.
      (definitely not)   1   _2_   3   4   5   (definitely)

What will happen during the coming week?

What will parent do?   _I will phone Mr. Zapata and ask him to send a report home about Felix._

What will child do?   _I won't talk back to Mr. Zapata. I'll stop blaming others when I get in trouble._

What will consultant do?   _I will phone the counselor and tell her that you have followed through on her referral._

Next conference date _10/7_   Time _6:15 p.m._

Victor's consistent support of Linda's authority is evident in this dialogue from a subsequent session:

Victor -- Do you have a VCR? (Felix nods in the affirmative.) Then you could get your homework done first the way your mother wants you to and still watch your show.

Felix -- Yeah, I could record it.

Victor -- Yes, you could, but only if you got your mom's okay and worked out the details with her.

The above dialogue also illustrates the gains that can be made simply by having the parent present. The advantages of a consultative approach are apparent when one compares the case of Felix to that of Sam described at the beginning of the chapter.

Forging an agreement between Felix and Linda and Mr. Zapata was a delicate task. First, Victor got Felix to list classroom events that made him angry. Buried in a sea of gripes (e.g., "Mr. Zapata took my pencil away for nothing.") were some reasonable complaints that Victor would bring to Mr. Zapata as suggestions: "Stop coming to my table and looking over my shoulder," and "Give me more time to finish my work." Victor framed his suggestions as an experiment that would be reevaluated on a weekly basis. Under those conditions, Mr. Zapata agreed to give Felix some "space" and a fresh start. Mr. Zapata said, however, that he was tired of the way that Felix was always getting a break.

When Linda phoned Mr. Zapata and arranged for reports to be sent home, the groundwork was laid for a working relationship. Victor had to make sure that the reports from the teacher reached their intended destination. If Felix were to keep "losing" his teacher reports, the mother might well have given up on the entire procedure and the teacher given up on the parent. Felix was rewarded for merely bringing the report home and, conversely, received a negative consequence for a missing report. Felix was told when the contract was agreed upon that the consequence for a missing report would be greater than the consequence for a bad report. Otherwise, Felix would have an incentive to lose any bad reports.

Disengagement. This is the "wind down" of the consultation process. The consultant reviews the target behaviors that have been achieved since the first session. The degree of success is

29

assessed and the degree of failure, if any, acknowledged. The consultant prepares the family for the likelihood of some backsliding but predicts a swift recovery should backsliding occur by noting maxims such as, "It is human nature to take two steps backwards for three forward." In Felix' case, a celebration was in order. All of the target goals were accomplished to a significant degree.

Implications for Practice

This case illustrates the importance of the voluntary nature of consultation. Most parents would likely benefit from experiencing consultation. But unless they freely volunteer to be consultees, little progress is likely to be made in consultation. Consequently, it is important for human service consultants to actively market consultation services so that their services are viewed as positive, useful, desirable and non-threatening.

This case shows how consultation is typically brief. By carefully planning the structure and process of consultation, consultants can make maximum benefit of their contact with consultees. It is the quality of the time spent with the consultee that is essential. This is particularly important for school-based consultants who must work within the confines of the school schedule and programs such as the Parent Consultation Center.

The nature of the Parent Consultation Center demonstrates the importance of clear expectations regarding what consultation can and cannot accomplish. It is important for referral sources to understand who consultation is for so that inappropriate referrals are not made. Consultees need to understand what consultation is all about so they can "buy into" the process as well as obtain the most benefit.

The point of view of brief family consultation, that counselors should consult with a child's "significant others," has received substantial support in recent publications (Beal & Chertkov, 1992; Fine, 1992; Gerler, 1993; Hinkle, 1993; Lambie & Daniels-Mohring, 1993; Nicoli, 1992; Ritchie & Partin, 1994). The use of brief family consultation at the Parent Consultation Center provides a working model for anyone who wishes to put this concept into action.

Further, this case points out the importance of collaboration in the consultation process. Through collaboration, the consultant empowers the adult significant others in the child's life as well as the child him- or herself. Through such collaboration, the family will be better able to deal with future problem situations. Collaboration is also essential in that it is a tool by which the consultant can assist the family in taking "ownership" of the problem at hand. Such ownership reduces the potential for resistance from family members as well as the risk of premature termination of the consultation relationship by one or more family members.

This approach also illustrates the importance of having the parties involved in consultation understand that the payoffs for participating in the process outweigh the "costs" of change. The case of Felix clearly was a difficult one. If the consultant had not helped the family see the benefits of change, it is unlikely that Felix and his family would have accepted much assistance.

References and Suggested Readings

Beal, E. W., & Chertkov, L. S. (1992). Family-school intervention: A family systems perspective. In M. Fine and C. Carlson (Eds.), The handbook of family-school intervention: A system perspective (pp. 288-310). Boston: Allyn & Bacon.

Bergan, J. R., & Kratochwill, T. R. (1990). Behavioral consultation and therapy. New York: Plenum Press.

Fine, M. J. (1992). A systems-ecological perspective on home-school intervention. In M. Fine and C. Carlson (Eds.), The handbook of family-school intervention: A systems perspective (pp. 1-17). Boston: Allyn & Bacon.

Gerler, E. R. (1993). Parents, families, and the schools. Elementary School Guidance & Counseling, 27, 243-244.

Golden, L. (1988). Quick assessment of family functioning. School Counselor, 35, 179-184.

Hinkle, J. S. (1993). Training school counselors to do family counseling. Elementary School Guidance & Counseling, 27, 252-257.

Kratochwill, T. R., & Bergan, J. R. (1990). Behavioral consultation in applied settings. New York: Plenum Press.

Lambie, R., & Daniels-Mohring, D. (1993). Family systems within educational contexts: Understanding students with special needs. Denver: Love.

Nicoli, W. G. (1992). A family counseling and consultation model for school counselors. School Counselor, 39, 351-361.

Ritchie, M. H., & Partin, R. L. (1994). Parent education and consultation activities of school counselors. School Counselor, 41, 165-170.

Editor's Note: Now that you have read this case, reflect upon it and develop a list of five things you might have done differently if you were a consultant involved with the case.

CHAPTER THREE

ADLERIAN PARENT CONSULTATION

Jon Carlson

Setting and Background Issues

Setting. This consultation took place in a private mental health clinic. The clinic is located in an affluent resort area on the west coast. The clinic's clients are composed of upper middle class families who often spend winters in their second homes in the area. There is also a large population of people who work in service and tourism industries in the area. The case below describes an Adlerian approach to parent consultation.

Background. Tom and Judy were concerned about their 10-year-old daughter Erin. At the time of this consultation she was in the fourth grade at the local public school. Erin has one brother, Scott, age 4. Erin was having a negative year at school and did not seem to like her teacher.

However, she was doing very well academically at school and had a lot of friends. Her most obvious symptoms were crying whenever she had to separate from her parents. Her mother described Erin as very sensitive and emotional, just like herself

33

and Erin's maternal grandmother and great-grandmother. Erin's maternal family was very close to her and to one another, while her father reported minimal contact with his family. It appears as though Erin was her mother's understudy. Erin had been diagnosed with precocious puberty, a condition in which puberty began for her at age 8.

Judy reported that their major concerns with Erin were crying, worries about homework, moodiness, unhappiness, and allergies. Erin had had regular physical exams and that was how the precocious puberty and allergies for molds were diagnosed. At the time of this consultation she was taking antibiotic medications for severe acne. Erin frequently had an upset stomach, an excessive appetite, and some temper control problems. On the physical side, Erin was considerably overweight. Socially, Erin had no trouble and reported many friends at school. Her father, a local restaurant owner, was seldom home. Her mother, a special education teacher in a neighboring school district, was the primary caregiver in the family.

Erin reported being very close to her maternal grandparents who lived next door. She was also close to her maternal aunt and great-grandmother who lived down the street. Erin reported no contact whatsoever with the paternal side of her family. It is interesting to note that both mom, grandmother, aunt, and great-grandmother cried frequently, sometimes on a daily basis.

The presenting problem the parents mentioned was Erin's negative year at school and the fact that she did not like her teacher. Despite doing well at school, Erin cried each morning when her father took her to school and she didn't want to leave the car to go into the school.

Consultation Goals

1. Improve Erin's self-understanding and self-acceptance.
2. Identify the goal of Erin's misbehavior.
3. Reduce Erin's crying and unhappiness.
4. Assist the parents in developing more effective parenting skills.
5. Reduce enmeshment in the maternal family of origin.

Consultation Function and Role

In this case, Erin's father (Tom) and mother (Judy) sought out this psychologist at the mental health clinic. The original idea was that I would work directly with Erin in a counseling relationship aimed at helping her at school. Tom, Judy and Erin came for a first session. Once the necessary forms were filled out, the intake session began. Each person was asked to describe their view of and historical perspective on Erin's crying and her unhappiness at school. As the family members discussed these issues, it became apparent to me that it would be best to work with Erin in individual counseling and at the same time develop a consultation relationship with the parents. The family concluded, and I agreed, that Erin would be better off working with me to control her crying behavior and secondarily to improve her situation at school. Although family therapy might certainly have been appropriate, I chose not to go in this direction. Through the use of individual counseling and parent consultation, Erin would hopefully receive the help she needed and the parents could work together to provide Erin the support she needed at home. I felt that there was some enmeshment in the maternal family that would be reduced by working with both parents in a consultation relationship. By bringing the mother and father together as a team, the enmeshment between Erin and her mother (and the extended maternal family)

35

would hopefully be correspondingly reduced. The parents agreed to a three session consultation relationship and I was to see Erin in individual counseling as long as necessary to meet the goals of counseling. For the purposes of this paper, I will focus only on the consultation relationship with Erin's parents.

Consultee Experience in Consultation

Neither parent had experienced a consultation relationship before. The parents reported that Erin periodically saw the school counselor as a result of her crying behavior. However, these visits seemed to occur only occasionally and on a crisis basis. Both parents seemed eager to meet in this setting and were willing to do anything necessary to help Erin. As the father noted: "I love Erin to death but at the same time her behavior is causing the family a great deal of stress. We need to do something and do it now!"

The parents functioned in the role of "students" as I outlined and discussed some of the principles of Adlerian psychology. They then became active problem solvers in their attempts to become more effective parents and assist Erin with the changes she agreed to work on during her counseling sessions with me.

Application: Consultant Techniques and Procedures

Entry. In the entry level meeting (as I have noted) it seemed important to work directly with both of these motivated parents. By having both of them describe the problem from their eyes, the importance of their being separate individuals would be stressed. At the same time it would allow me to assist them in becoming a team in their work with Erin. I also thought that such an effort would reduce some of the enmeshment I noted between the mother and daughter (as well as in the extended maternal family) at the intake session.

Diagnosis. The basic presenting problem for the parents was that they wanted to help Erin work on her crying and unhappiness. "She has so much going for her. We just can't understand why she acts this way," said the mother. From the Adlerian/psychodynamic perspective, it appears as though the paternal family was disengaged and the maternal family enmeshed, with Erin finding her attention and place in the family through inappropriate use of emotions. From this assessment it became important that Erin learn new ways to find appropriate attention, as well as to disengage herself from her maternal family and make contact with her paternal family. It seemed important to address that crying was a family value. If the parents could assist Erin in reducing her crying and at the same time help her to develop more positive ways to gain attention within the immediate and extended families, then the parents would be effectively complementing my work with Erin in our counseling relationship.

Implementation. Session One. As I have noted above, the first session was the initial interview and assessment with Tom, Judy and Erin. At that time the parents agreed to three consultation sessions and Erin agreed to individual counseling with me. During this first meeting, I indirectly pointed out that Erin wanted very badly to be an adult and to individuate. However, I was of the opinion that no one in the maternal family had ever completed this task. I cautioned the family that Erin's crying was most likely a function of the family's interaction and that we might have to have Erin and the family do some "funny" things to change her crying and unhappiness.

Session Two. In this session I provided the parents with a copy of Dinkmeyer and McKay's (1973) Raising a responsible child. I suggested they pay particular attention to the sections on the goals of misbehavior and differentiating when the adult has the problem from when the child has the problem. In order to attack the problem of crying, I asked the parents, in a fun and low-key fashion, to encourage Erin to practice her crying behavior daily.

37

By sanctioning crying in this paradoxical fashion, the family rules would most likely begin to change. Further, I informed the parents that if they responded differently to Erin's crying behavior than they did currently, then she would be more likely to seek a more age-appropriate way of obtaining positive attention from the adult significant others in her life. So I suggested that during the first week, the parents should ask Erin to cry for five minutes per day at home. During the second week Erin would be asked to cry ten minutes per day at home. I encouraged the parents to praise Erin for how well she was crying. Here is some sample dialogue to demonstrate some of what happened in this session:

Consultant:	Judy and Tom, I would like each of you to describe how you react when Erin cries at home.
Judy:	I get really upset that Erin cries every morning. It upsets Tom as he's going to work. The teacher and other school personnel also get concerned. In spite of this, she does very well in school.
Consultant:	Tom?
Tom:	Well, I know I get upset and tend to reassure and coddle her. I just want to get her to school peacefully so that I can get on with my work at the restaurant. I guess it would be very convenient for us to blame her teacher and the school, but realistically, I think we're going to have to treat this crying business differently at home.
Judy:	That's right.
Consultant:	Judy, during our last session you said that Erin is just too sensitive and emotional just like you think you are.
Judy:	That's right. I guess I learned this crying business from my mother and grandmother. They also cry a lot too.
Consultant:	I think that Erin's goal here is to get attention from you two as well as demonstrate that she's not quite "okay." I think she sees it as just having a real

	difficult time each morning. I am not sure whether she believes she has any control over her crying. She feels just fine as long as she's at home or with her grandparents.
Judy:	That's it in a nutshell.
Consultant:	I know this might sound a little silly, since we're trying to eliminate Erin's crying behavior, but a lot of times the reason we can't solve problems is that we're doing things backwards. It's been my experience that the best way to stop a problem like this is to practice it and to truly get control of it.
Judy and Tom (at the same time):	
	You mean, you want us to encourage Erin to practice crying?
Consultant:	Yes, that's exactly right. I'd like you to have her practice crying for five minutes each day this week, and then ten minutes each day the following week. I'd like for you to have her practice crying in order to really get control over it. I think once she learns how to start it and stop it, things will go much easier for everyone at home, with the relatives and at school.

<u>Session Three</u>. Judy and Tom reported that Erin had been much better about not crying in the morning and had actually been much better overall during the last two weeks. Erin seemed to be able to control her crying much better. During this session, I asked the parents to discuss the differences in the families of origin. As the discussion progressed, I pointed out that Tom's family was detached and Judy's family was quite enmeshed. I pointed out that if the parents could increase contact for Erin with Tom's family and correspondingly decrease contact with Judy's family, then the modeling for the crying by the maternal family of origin might be neutralized. At this time I also reviewed the Adlerian concept of encouragement and helped the parents plan to apply it as they switched the amount of contact time Erin was going to have with

39

her relatives. A plan was made that reduced Erin's contact with the maternal side of the family to one day per week (with Erin choosing the day). The dialogue below illustrates how this was accomplished.

Consultant: How have things been going?

Judy: Erin has been much better about not crying in the morning. Actually, she's been much better overall throughout the last two weeks.

Tom: Yes. She's been crying a lot less, only once, maybe twice that I can remember. I tease her when she gets out of the car at school. I say: "One more cry for old time's sake." She just laughs and smiles.

Consultant: Are you still instructing Erin to cry as we had agreed upon?

Tom: I don't know if she needs to practice crying any more. She seems to be doing OK and has much better control over the crying now.

Consultant: I get the feeling that part of this problem comes from the fact that Erin is too close to you (Judy) and her grandparents, and that even though Erin would like to grow up and be an adult, the role modeling she receives makes that difficult.

Judy: I see what you're saying. Erin sort of practices what she sees all of us doing, like the crying bit.

Consultant: My guess is that you are correct. Erin lives right next door to her grandparents and talks with them several times a day, as well as with her aunt and her grandmother. It seems as though Erin has too much contact with your family, Judy, but not enough with yours, Tom.

Judy: I see your point. I guess Erin can't learn how to grow up when she sees all of that crying.

Consultant: With that in mind, what I'd like to suggest is that you significantly limit Erin's contact with your

	family, Judy. At the same time, Tom, I recommend that you increase Erin's contact with your family.
Tom:	That's probably a good point. At least Erin will get a balanced perspective from having contact with my relatives. It's not that we're not close. It's just that my family is so work oriented that we spend very little time together. Since my dad's death last year we hardly communicate except during the holidays.
Consultant:	Tom, I know you're saying that your family is not perfect either. But as you said: in this situation a balanced perspective might well be in Erin's best interest.

Session Four. I met with the parents two weeks after session three. Things were reportedly going the same, with little or no crying by Erin the previous week. Tom had contacted his family and had taken Erin over to see her grandmother in a town twenty miles away. Tom reported that the visit went quite well and that Erin had talked all the way home about how the grandmother was going to teach her how to crochet "granny squares." Judy reported that the contact with the maternal family had been limited considerably; however, no one appeared very happy about this situation. Both parents reported, however, that they were still one hundred percent behind the idea.

At this point I felt confident that the crying behavior was under control. As her crying had decreased so had Erin's "unhappiness" at school. As I talked with the parents they asked for more assistance in developing more effective parenting skills. Based on my impressions of the family I believed they could benefit from a parenting style that would make Erin more independent. To confirm this hypothesis, I asked Judy and Tom to describe a typical day beginning with the morning on through the rest of the day regarding how they related to Erin. It became increasing clear that both parents, but Judy in particular, were taking excessive responsibility for reminding Erin to complete her chores and

41

homework. In some cases, Judy was doing the chores and some of the homework for Erin. I thought to myself: "no wonder this child loves the home and hates the school. She has to *work* at school!"

I then introduced the parents to the Adlerian ideas about logical and natural consequences. I suggested that homework would now be Erin's responsibility and the parents were not to comment on it. It was further suggested that the parents not remind Erin to complete any of her chores. For example, rather than put Erin's clothes away, the parents would simply take them and place them in the laundry bag. If Erin wanted to wear any of the clothes she would have to wash and dry them herself first. The final portion of this session dealt with humor and how the entire family might benefit from learning how to "chill out" more. The ensuing discussion and planning session resulted in some possible ways for the parents to encourage play and fun in the family. The dialogue below is taken from this fourth session.

Consultant:	What's been different since our last visit?
Judy:	Things have been going just about the same. Last week there was no crying, but Erin did have one little spell this morning right before school.
Consultant:	Everyone seems to be making great strides. How have you done in terms of dealing with your families?
Tom:	We haven't talked very much at all to either of them, maybe only once or twice this past week.
Consultant:	That sounds great. How are you helping Erin to be more responsible at home?
Judy:	What do you mean?
Consultant:	Let's go through your description of what a typical day is like for Erin, starting with waking up in the morning.
Consultant (after the description by parents):	
	Well Tom and Judy, it seems as though you're working overtime.

42

Judy:	What do you mean?
Tom:	Yeah, help me with that. I don't get where you're going.
Consultant:	Well, it appears as though both of you are doing many things that Erin can do for herself. One of the things I mentioned in one of our first sessions was the cardinal rule of parenting: not to do anything for somebody that they can do for themselves. I wonder what would happen if you backed off on her homework and stopped reminding her and stopped putting her clothes away, etc. (I then discussed in detail natural and logical consequences and differentiating when an adult has the problem from when the child has the problem.)
Tom:	I guess you're right on this one. I like the idea of Erin doing more for herself. Heck, that means more free time and less stress for me!
Judy:	Well, I don't know that she would do it.
Consultant:	Yes, that is a common concern of parents in your position. But let me encourage you to try some of these things. Maybe if you act as if they will work, then they will.
Judy:	Well, I think we should start with the chores at home. That way we can free a lot of time for ourselves and help Erin be more responsible at the same time.
Consultant:	One of the interesting things I've noticed from working with both of you is that you both use very little emotion and fun as you talk and describe situations at home. My guess is that being in your family is not fun, but more of a chore. I'm wondering if you've noticed this.
Judy:	You're right. We don't laugh and joke around much.
Consultant:	I'm interested in seeing if the two of you would generate some more ways to approach life in a more

	playful and fun fashion, rather than being so serious all of the time.
Judy and Tom:	What could we do?
Consultant:	I believe that perhaps your family has forgotten how to have fun. Let's put our heads together and see what we can come up with.

At this point I went into teaching the steps of problem-solving in which Judy and Tom could clearly see what options they had and how they had not been choosing them.

Disengagement. A follow-up phone call two weeks later indicated that Erin was doing much better. The family was experiencing little negative emotion, no crying, and some fun.

I suggested that no further sessions needed to be scheduled at this time and asked the parents to set up an appointment in six months for a follow up session.

Implications for Practice

One implication of this case for practice is that consultation can involve teaching. The parents were motivated but lacking in awareness of some very basic parenting strategies. Consequently, I shared a text on parenting with them as well as taking time during our consultation sessions to instruct them in how to use Adlerian parenting strategies with Erin.

This case also illustrates how parents can use, with a consultant's guidance, some deceptively simple interventions with some rather dramatic effects. Using a more traditional therapeutic model, either Erin would have been seen alone for weekly play therapy with minimum parental involvement or possibly sessions with the entire family would have been conducted. It is unlikely that the former would have had much impact on the situation; however, the latter would probably work. However, it would have been much more costly. Through the use of brief, short-term consultation and individual counseling with the child, a systemic second order change occurred, one in which the presenting problems were also appropriately modified.

The key to successful consultation with parents seems to be in the ability to effectively assess the presenting problem and context in order to formulate a multi-faceted treatment plan. The presenting problem of being unhappy with school did not fit with the description of being a good student and getting along with friends. It was important to identify the purpose/goal of this behavior. Careful questioning involving relationships between the family members uncovered a goal of attention-getting on one level and a learned family pattern on another. The interventions involved sanctioning the crying behavior and actually asking that it occur. This simple suggestion changed the relationship dynamics and made crying much less effective as a means of gaining attention.

Another implication for practice is that consultants may need to do more in parent consultation than assist the parents in changing the child's behavior. In this case, the suggestions of changing the amount and type of contact with both families of origin were made in order to disrupt the overly enmeshed/overly detached pattern. An effective family communication structure was developed by limiting Erin's contact with her maternal grandparents, increasing contact with the father's family, having the parents not do things for Erin that she could do for herself, and having the parents work on adding a more humorous element to the family atmosphere.

A final implication involves risk-taking. By having a strong relationship with consultees, consultants can take calculated risks which can expedite the consultation process. In this particular case, the consultant risked suggesting that the parents change their family's interaction pattern with the maternal and paternal families of origin.

References and Suggested Readings

Dinkmeyer, D., Jr., Carlson, J., Dinkmeyer, D., Sr. (1994). Consultation: School mental health professionals as consultants. Muncie, IN: Accelerated Development.

Dinkmeyer, D., & McKay, G. (1973). Raising a responsible child: Practical steps for effective family relationships. New York: Simon and Schuster.

Sherman, R., & Dinkmeyer, D., Sr. (1987). Systems of family therapy: An Adlerian integration. New York: Brunner/Mazel.

Editor's Note: Now that you have read this case, reflect upon it and develop a list of five things you might have done differently if you were a consultant involved with this case.

CHAPTER FOUR

EDUCATION/TRAINING CONSULTATION WITH

SCHOOL PERSONNEL

Mary D. Deck and Glenda Isenhour

Setting and Background Issues

<u>Setting</u>. As counselor educators, we were contacted to be
consultants for a large school system and asked to provide a two-
day in-service for teachers, school counselors, and administrators.
The in-service was one component of a grant-funded project
targeted at designing interventions for assisting at-risk students to
remain in school. The primary purpose of the in-service was to
educate the participants on how to develop strategies for working
with these at-risk students. Teams, consisting of a teacher,
counselor and an administrator from each school in the system
were invited to be participants. Upon completion of the two-day
in-service training, each school team was to develop and conduct a
similar in-service program with their particular faculty and staff to
develop strategies for assisting at-risk students. Given this
"training-to-be-trainers" concept, the participants in our in-service
were initially consultees and would subsequently become trainers
and internal consultants in their own schools.

47

The school system in which the consultation occurred serves a county with a population of approximately 90,000. The county is the central retail and medical center for a relatively urban metropolitan area of approximately 250,000 people. Twenty public schools comprise the school system. Thirteen schools are elementary with either grades kindergarten through fifth or kindergarten through eighth. There are three middle schools serving grades sixth through eighth and four high schools serving grades ninth through twelfth. The schools' enrollments range from approximately 350 students in four of the smaller elementary schools to approximately 1,300 students in the largest high school. Sixteen of the schools have at least one full-time school counselor, and the four smaller elementary schools have a counselor on a half-time basis. These same four elementary schools do not have assistant principals. The racial and ethnic descriptions of the student population vary considerably based on the geographical location of the school.

Background. One issue that concerned us was the fact that we were university professors and that this fact could automatically prejudice the consultees against the in-service. In our heads, we could hear such comments as: "Oh, no. One more in-service!" "I don't have time for some 'expert' to lecture me about kids. What do they know about at-risk kids?" "I have too much to do to waste two days listening to someone tell me how to do something that won't work here." We were aware these are often expressed or unexpressed sentiments of school personnel required to attend in-service and staff development programs. These had, in fact, been our reactions too on occasions when we felt forced or coerced to be consultees in staff training. Too often the perception of consultees is that in-service means sitting through lectures, evaluations, or criticisms from people removed from the "real work experience," or as one of our colleagues says, people who do not have "dirty hands." We knew if we ignored such perceptions and attitudes we were fostering resistance. Even the most valuable information and training can be lost when the consultees involved

48

in an educational and training consultation are not acknowledged for their own expertise and are not invited to engage in the exchange of information. We were cognizant that we needed to recognize that our consultees were adult learners who already possessed expertise and that we needed to help them feel empowered and confident to return to their schools and share that expertise. Therefore, we wanted them to be able to access and share their own wealth of information, particularly about the nature of at-risk students and what strategies might work for them. In addition we wanted to help them feel a sense of connection and personalization with the training experience itself.

A related concern was how to help the consultees interact, share, and work with one another to problem-solve and develop strategies for helping at-risk students. We were aware that we were bringing together a diverse group of individuals. Since all schools in the system would likely be involved, there would be persons present with vested interests and questions about at-risk students from kindergarten through high school. With the school teams representing teachers, counselors, and administrators, these professionals would bring differing perspectives and objectives. There was also the potential for some consultees to be intimidated by having administrators who were their immediate supervisors participate, especially when everyone would be asked to identify areas for improvement and offer suggestions for change. We recognized that to help our consultees build cohesion and readiness for working together, we needed to structure the in-service using group development principles, group process skills, and the nominal group technique. We decided that our entire in-service would be designed to facilitate the consultees' movement through the levels of group development. We chose to use a group development model developed by Merritt and Walley (1977). By utilizing a group problem-solving approach, we trusted we would enhance the solicitation of information from consultees and also model for them a format they could employ when they designed their own in-service for use at their individual schools.

As we considered some of the design and process issues for preparing this in-service, we also considered content issues. Consultation that is educational and training based is, by the nature of its purpose, built upon content and information. We wanted consultees to share their expertise, but we also needed to examine what additional information on working with at-risk students would be relevant and important for us to present for discussion and training purposes. We focused our preparation through reading and literature reviews on at-risk students and school drop outs (e.g., Cuban, 1989; Fine, 1988; Hamby, 1989; Peck, Law, & Mills, 1987; Slavin & Madden, 1989).

Consultation Goals

When contacted to provide this in-service, we were being asked to provide consultation through education and training. This type of consultation is the most common form of the purchase of expertise model of consultation (Dougherty, 1995). The consultation can be exclusively educationally and didactically based, such as when the consultant provides information through a formal presentation or lecture. On the other hand, the consultant may be more of a trainer, focusing primarily on experiential learning and assisting the consultees in the acquisition and rehearsal of skills.

Our goal was to combine both education and training. One education goal was to disseminate information and provide resource materials to enhance the knowledge base and confidence levels of our consultees. Another education goal was to expand the purchase of expertise model to include opportunities for the consultees to be the experts; that is, to educate one another about helping at-risk students. We wanted to create an environment in which the information and expertise that the consultees brought to the in-service could be tapped and shared with others. We also wanted considerable experiential learning to occur so that our modeling and training efforts would transfer into the behavioral repertoire of the consultees. Another training goal was to have consultees participate in group activities that would engage them in meaningful interaction with each other. Our overriding goals were for consultees to leave the in-service having been respected for their knowledge and expertise and having had opportunities to experience personalized learning. Meeting these goals would assist consultees in their individual interactions with students and parents and would provide information and experiences they could transfer when designing their own in-service program.

Consultant Function and Roles

As education/training consultants, our primary function was to design and execute an in-service that would meet the expectations and intent of the funding source for the in-service, meet the needs of the consultees as participants in the in-service and as future trainers and best utilize our strengths, skills, and knowledge as consultants.

We determined that it was essential for the consultees to understand group development and the dynamics of group process if they were to be trainers themselves. They needed to appreciate and understand experientially how to problem-solve using the steps involved in group development and group process. Our role was to design strategies that focused on meeting the needs of at-risk students. At the same time, we needed to align the sequence and presentation of the strategies directly with the steps in building a group. Once we solidified this notion of linking content, training, and group development, we structured the total in-service on a group development model (Merritt & Walley, 1977).

Another tool that our consultees needed was familiarity with the nominal group technique (NGT) (Delbecq, Van de Ven, & Gustafson, 1975). Employing NGT would further strengthen our supposition that all consultees possessed useful information and experiences. NGT emphasizes the value of each individual's

51

contributions. Using NGT was also part of our trainer role, encouraging consultees to experience techniques and tools they might incorporate into their own in-service delivery model.

Another aspect of our educator role was compiling a handbook for consultees. We included information on the following topics: steps in group development; nominal group technique procedures; self-concept, self-esteem, and school performance; effective communication; parent-school partnerships; bibliography on at-risk students and drop-out prevention; and a step-by-step reference guide detailing the entire two-day in-service (i.e., agenda, timelines, and directions for activities and copies of all handouts). This handbook was to be a primer for the consultees as they prepared for their own in-service.

In planning for the in-service, we also moved into our role of evaluator. We developed an evaluation instrument designed to assess both content and experiential goals and objectives of the in-service. The instrument included 23 Likert-scale items and five open-ended response items. The school system added one item which asked how the central office staff might help the consultees prepare and conduct a similar in-service in their schools.

Consultees' Experience in Consultation

In working with the grant director in planning the logistics of the in-service, we requested that the in-service be on two consecutive days. We thought that the concentrated time would increase the momentum and effect of the group development process. We wanted to maintain the energy level and involvement that we felt would be created the first day.

To promote the in-service, the grant director made a brief presentation to the principals during one of their meetings with the superintendent. The superintendent endorsed the in-service and

52

stressed the administrative commitment to this project. With the project director, we helped draft a letter and develop an information packet for prospective participants. The principals were to distribute these materials to those who indicated interest. In this letter, we emphasized the voluntary nature of the in-service. A goal and purpose statement was included to ensure that those who volunteered were willing to be trainers later in their own schools. We also highlighted the experiential nature of the in-service. We hoped to encourage participation by consultees who would be in agreement with and supportive of the goals of the in-service. We also requested that volunteers commit to attending both days of the in-service. We explained that due to the experiential nature of the in-service, it would diminish the impact for everyone if someone had to be absent for part of the experience.

Incentives for consultees included substitute pay for the two days, catered lunch for both days, a video tape with a resource packet on working with parents of at-risk students, continuing education credits and a certificate of attendance.

Application: Consultation Techniques and Procedures

Entry. During the summer, we were contacted by an administrator from the central office of a large school system who asked if we were interested in leading an in-service for teachers, counselors, and administrators. The in-service was one part of a fairly extensive grant that was being written to focus on drop-out prevention. We agreed that we would work with the school system to develop such an in-service if funding became available. Major goals for the in-service, possible numbers of participants and training dates, availability of resources, and payment for consultation services were discussed during this initial contact. No further contact was made until mid-fall when the administrator contacted us to inform us that the grant had been funded and that they were in the process of hiring a director to administer the grant. When a director was employed, we would finalize plans for the in-service.

In early December, we were contacted by the director of the grant. Our initial meeting was in mid-December at the school system's central office and lasted for about an hour. At this meeting, we clarified expectations and goals for the in-service, explored possible dates, discussed the necessity for committed volunteers who understood fully the expectation to be trainers upon completion of the in-service, reviewed preliminary ideas for using steps in group development as the foundation for the delivery of the in-service, and discussed the kind of facility that would be needed. Because this grant project had several facets, a number of resource materials had been purchased for the consultees. During this initial meeting, we were introduced to the school superintendent and other central office administrators. Before leaving, we scheduled a half-day work session with the grant director for early January.

Much of the half-day session was devoted to discussion about the structure of and logistical planning for the in-service. We knew that as many as ninety participants might attend. It was decided that the in-service would be located in the system's central office in a large multi-purpose room which had sufficient open space with portable chairs so consultees could easily work in dyads, triads, small groups of 10 or less, and also assemble in a large circle. We also spent some time discussing the handbook and evaluation instrument that we, the consultants, would develop and deadlines for printing these items. We drafted the letter and information sheets that would be distributed to the principals for recruiting consultees. We established the dates for the in-service in early May. The in-service would occur after the annual system-wide testing and prior to the final crunch of the end-of-school activities.

We left feeling the meeting had been very productive and that we were now able to plan the remaining details of the in-service.

Diagnosis. Entering this stage, we had already read the grant, completed our reading of the literature review, and gathered additional information from the grant director about the system's expectations. We knew the overall goals of the in-service, and we had defined some of our concerns about the in-service, e.g., to recruit volunteers, to build the in-service around stages of group development, etc. Our task now was to design the in-service and to develop specific tasks, strategies, and timelines for the implementation of the in-service. We needed to design a systematic approach that linked experiences in group development and group process with relevant content for addressing the needs of at-risk students. To do this, we had three main areas to consider: what model of group development would meet our goals, what content areas needed to be presented, and what activities and strategies would incorporate group development steps as well as focus on at-risk students.

First, we considered models of group development and chose to adopt and modify the steps suggested by Merritt and Walley (1977). The steps of interest and involvement, participation, cohesion and harmony, self-disclosure, critical thinking, problem identification, and problem solving met our goals of encouraging the consultees to become acquainted with one another, sharing existing information and expertise, and gradually moving them to brainstorming and creative problem solving. Once we had the structural model for group development, we had an outline for developing the specifics of the in-service.

We thought it necessary to include limited amounts of didactic information. We brainstormed about content areas that might be included. We then prioritized content areas, selecting these four main areas to emphasize: considerations for working with groups, self-concept and self-esteem, invitational learning, and communication skills. We would provide brief overviews of each of these topics and intersperse experiential learning in the presentations.

It seemed that the majority of the in-service should be spent in experiential learning. We brainstormed about the type of content activities and strategies we might employ at each of the group development steps. We then selected those strategies that seemed to best fit the group development step <u>and</u> foster content learning. We were now ready to construct the in-service format, including timelines, materials, and resources needed.

When we had completed the above procedures, we then developed the instrument to evaluate the in-service and compiled and organized the materials for the handbook. We also made a materials checklist (e.g., newsprint, markers, overheads, notecards, etc.) which we submitted to the project director.

We met again with the project director to present the outline for the in-service, collaborate on additions and changes to the evaluation instrument, and to make final requests for materials and resources for the in-service. At that time, we also heard from the director about possible glitches regarding consultee participation for the in-service. For example, some principals were not recruiting but were requiring certain staff to attend and a few who really wanted to attend could only be present the second day. We discussed contingencies for handling such concerns within the framework of the in-service. We strongly discouraged the director from including persons who could only attend one day, and particularly only the second day, because of the emphasis on group development as a training model. (As it turned out, four participants were able to attend the first day only, and on the second day, there were no new participants.)

<u>Implementation</u>. The in-service was scheduled on a Wednesday and Thursday beginning at 8:30 in the morning and ending by 3:30

each afternoon. There were eighty consultees participating on Wednesday and seventy-six on Thursday. All of the twenty schools in the system had at least one staff person in attendance. Most schools had their three-person team.

Below, we outline the two-day proceedings by including a brief description of each of the experiential strategies used (labeled Strategy) and explaining how each strategy also corresponded to meeting one or more of the steps in the group development process (labeled Intent). At the points where we presented content information, we also provide a brief overview of what occurred.

Day 1. Interest and Involvement: Get-Acquainted, Self-Esteem Strategy. Following registration and distribution of materials, we moved immediately into an experiential "get-acquainted" activity. This activity encouraged the participants to describe themselves in terms of four conditions of self-esteem and also met the first two steps of group development, interest and involvement. We participated in this activity with the consultees.

Involvement and Participation: Sharing Expertise and Knowledge about At-Risk Students. Following the get-acquainted exercise, we spent an hour in a small group activity where consultees identified characteristics, feelings, and needs of at-risk students and their parents and current school responses to these needs. We facilitated this activity but did not join in the small groups' generation of information.

Intent: Involvement and participation are enhanced using small groups, assigning structured tasks, and providing clear instructions. The activities are generally focused on identifying content problems as perceived by each member of the small group. By providing a specific task and asking for each person's content-related perception, an atmosphere conducive for sharing, listening and accepting of others' ideas develops.

Strategy: Consultees were randomly divided into small groups, given newsprint with markers, and assigned one or two specific questions from the following set of questions: Who are at-risk students? What are characteristics of at-risk students? How do teachers identify at-risk students in classes? What are needs of at-risk students? Which of these needs can be addressed within school? What are feelings and perceptions of at-risk students about school? How can these students' feelings and perceptions be altered? What are needs of parents of at-risk students? How can schools help meet the needs of these parents?

After generating responses to their particular questions, each small group reported its main ideas to the large group. For example, some of the reported characteristics of at-risk students were low self-esteem, acting out behaviors, few friends, and unkempt appearance. Some of the identified needs of at-risk students were to be successful, be accepted by school personnel, have someone listen and care, and have academic programs to meet their needs. After the group reports, we acknowledged and validated the consultees' expertise by linking the literature findings on dropout prevention and at-risk students to their first-hand experience and knowledge.

Cohesion and Harmony: Team Building. After the morning break, the consultees met in their school teams for thirty minutes and then in the larger group for forty-five minutes to discuss current strategies they were implementing in their individual schools to meet the needs of at-risk students. Throughout the in-service, when consultees met with their school teams, non-team participants met in triads to share ideas. The sharing of successful strategies focused everyone on the common goal of the in-service, strengthened the cohesion of the individual school teams, and created a network of resource persons from among the larger school system. We facilitated the large group discussion but did not participate in the earlier team discussions.

Intent: In order to experience cohesion and harmony, each consultee needs to feel he/she is an important, contributing member of the group (or team in this case). At this stage of group development, a sense of belongingness and unity of purpose binds group members together. Acceptance of one another, coupled with opportunities for listening and communicating, are both essential to the establishment of cohesion and harmony. Activities should encourage openness and foster teamwork through the sharing of ideas.

Strategy: The teacher, counselor and administrator from each school met as a team to discuss the strategies currently being used to meet the needs of at-risk students and their parents in their school. Each team then reported three of the strategies to the larger group. This activity focused the team on the identification of the positive aspects of their particular schools and then provided them an opportunity to hear ideas from other schools that might be replicated. This was a very uplifting and energizing experience as the teams were able to share the positive things they were doing and gather ideas for other interventions they might try.

Self-disclosure: Recalling and Sharing Personal School Experiences. The morning activities were relatively safe and non-threatening, focusing primarily on content information and revealing few differences of ideas or conflicting opinions. As the afternoon session began, we used an imagery exercise to move the consultees into more personal, self-revealing levels of exploration and sharing. We changed the focus from discussing external issues about students and their parents to examining more personal recollections of what it meant to each consultee to be a student. This experience was about a half hour in duration. One of us led the experience, and the other was a participant.

Intent: Self-disclosure is a pivotal point in group development as the consultees are asked to take more personal risks. An atmosphere characterized by trust and respect has been established, and consultees now begin sharing more personalized experiences,

59

beliefs, and feelings within the group. Self-sharing helps prepare consultees to engage in more critical, original, and divergent thinking and desensitizes fears about expressing personal ideas and opinions. Opportunities for self-disclosure help consultees clarify, question, and learn from others in a positive manner while valuing their own awarenesses and contributions. Activities designed to solicit self disclosures need to begin with topics requiring less personal disclosure and gradually move toward topics of a more personal nature. Not everyone will be ready for a deeper level of sharing, and the consultant needs to be sensitive to and respect their hesitancies.

Strategy: Consultees were led through a guided imagery exercise in which they were asked to visualize themselves as children in school and to remember experiences by responding to a series of questions related to invitational education and the development of self-esteem. The questions were: "How were you invited to learn in school? In what ways did you feel unique in school? How were you allowed to be in control and powerful in school? In what ways did you feel a sense of belongingness in school? Who were your adult role models in school?" Following the guided imagery exercise, each consultee was invited to share awarenesses from the exercise with a partner. Consultees could decline to share. After five minutes of mutual sharing, volunteers from the larger group were asked to share any thoughts or comments about their experience. This activity helped the consultees connect with their own childhood experiences related to school and personalize the conditions necessary for desiring to learn, feeling a part of the school, and developing self-esteem.

Content Presentation: Guidelines for Working with Groups. We blocked out an hour in mid-afternoon to briefly overview the steps in group development and relate them directly to the day's events. We had a worksheet that listed each of the earlier activities and the steps of group development. We also overviewed the following day's agenda and related it to group development. We included a

60

brainstorming session in which we asked participants to name important behaviors and traits for group leaders. We closed by referring consultees to the handbook and the display materials for additional information on working with groups.

Self-Disclosure: Experiencing Disinvitations. Another self-disclosure activity concluded the day's activities and set the stage for the following day. We gave a homework assignment to the consultees. One purpose of this assignment was to foster critical thinking and to encourage consultees to process what they had experienced during day one of the in-service. Another purpose was for the consultees to use their responses to the assignment for discussion on the following day.

Intent: The purpose of this activity was to place consultees in situations where they felt they did not belong and to have them share their feelings and responses to "being on the outside." We wanted consultees to leave mildly distressed in order to prompt their movement toward critical thinking and problem-identification. We thought if they "experienced" being disinvited and were left to ponder the experience, they would begin to consider ways to change similar "outside" experiences for at-risk students and their parents.

Strategy: The self-disclosure activity required the participants to break into groups of 10. Five persons formed a tight inner circle and five others formed an outer circle (Canfield & Wells, 1976). Persons within the inner circle selected a secret known only to the inner five. This secret was theirs to share or not to share with the outer circle members. Persons in the outer circle questioned, bargained, or pleaded with the inner circle members to learn the secret. After a few minutes, the circles were reversed and the same procedures were followed. Process questions followed the activity which allowed participants to express their feelings and perceptions when they were the inner circle member and when they were the outer circle member. As a homework assignment

61

participants were asked to consider how we disinvite others from belonging, from learning, from having control, and from feeling unique.

Assessment of Day 1. At the close of the in-service, we met for a few minutes with the project director to hear his assessment of the day. He stated that he was pleased with the interaction of the consultees and with the process. He thought that the strategies were adequately balanced between conveying content and providing for experiential learning. We also processed the day privately with each other. Overall, we were pleased with the way the day had progressed. We thought our goals were being met and that the strategies were being well-received. We were positive and eager to return the next day. We noted that one person in particular seemed to dominate whichever group she was in, that another had been rambling, long-winded, and somewhat judgmental about at-risk students in his responses, and that two persons were particularly reserved when we moved to the self-disclosure activities. We discussed interventions to address these concerns the following day.

Day 2. Most of the morning was devoted to content presentations with the infusion of some experiential components. The afternoon session was singularly focused on group work designed to identify innovative interventions to assist at-risk students and their parents. The experiential strategies of the previous day had served to introduce the day's topical presentations in a personal way to the consultees, and the group development steps had established a foundation of group cohesion and trust to move consultees to the working stage involving critical thinking, problem identification, and problem-solving.

Interest, Involvement, Participation, and Self-Disclosure: Self-Esteem Graffiti. We began the day with an experiential activity to help the consultees maintain the spirit and focus of the previous day. We participated fully in this activity.

Intent: This warm-up activity incorporated the group development steps of interest, involvement, participation, and self-disclosure. It was meant to center once more the consultees' attention on their own personal application of the four conditions of self-esteem.

Strategy: After the consultees signed in on the newsprint, they were asked to rotate to each of the other four newsprint sheets. They were to draw or use symbols to represent how each of the four conditions of self-esteem were being met in their lives. Each newsprint graffiti sheet was labeled with one of these four conditions of self-esteem: belongingness, personal power, uniqueness, and role model (Canfield & Wells, 1976; Clemes & Bean, 1980). After everyone had arrived and signed all the sheets, the entire group met in a circle, and each consultee re-introduced him or herself by sharing one response from the graffiti sheets. It was gratifying to us to watch the group of strangers from yesterday morning connecting today as they laughed and talked when signing the graffiti sheets.

Content Presentations: The Self, The Setting, and The Statements. The remainder of the morning session focused on the presentation and discussion of basic information from three theoretical approaches: self-concept/self-consistency (Hamachek, 1987), invitational learning (Purkey & Novak, 1984), and the facilitative model of communication (Myrick 1993; Witmer, 1992). We also used experiential approaches to supplement the information and to add to the personalization of the content. For example, to emphasize the interaction of self-concept and school achievement, we gave out self-concept labels to volunteers (e.g., teacher's pet, underachiever, shy child, etc.) and asked them to simulate a classroom setting and take on the behaviors that a student with that self-concept might engage in. We then had a short lesson with one of us role-playing the teacher. This improvisation proved to be one of the highlights of the morning. After the role-play, the group processed how each of the students saw themselves as a learner and how they felt about their place in the classroom and in school.

We also asked each of the role-play students to assess how at-risk they were for dropping out of school.

After the break, we examined invitational learning and the climate of the school setting. Based on the previous day's homework, we listed ways that schools and teachers communicate disinvitations to students and parents. We also explored effective communication as a key to invitational learning. To demonstrate a continuum of facilitative responses, one of us told an everyday story of misadventures (e.g., oversleeping, arriving late for a meeting, being in a traffic jam, etc.) and the consultees formulated statements that were helpful (e.g., understanding and empathic) or harmful (e.g., advice-giving and judgmental). We processed how these same kinds of responses are representative of what different students hear in school.

The experiential aspects of the content sessions allowed the consultees to remain active participants, to take risks (if they chose), and to share in the laughter and spontaneity of learning. Although the morning was very content laden, we felt that the pacing and weaving of experiential activities kept the presentation lively and personal.

Critical Thinking: Brainstorming Ways to Be More Invitational. The afternoon session began with consultees using the NGT techniques to generate ideas for being more invitational toward at-risk students and their parents. This experience was to create the broadest possible range of ideas for the school teams to consider later in the day when they were identifying possible new and innovative interventions that might be implemented in their schools. We facilitated the afternoon sessions, especially keeping track of time and focusing consultees to remain on task.

Intent: The critical thinking step of group development invites consultees to brainstorm and actively listen as others present their ideas. Consultees are offered opportunities to actively engage in

64

creative and original thinking. One of the critical rules of brainstorming is that all ideas are accepted without critique or evaluation. The consultant may need to reemphasize the need to accept and respect the ideas and contributions of others. One way to encourage critical thinking and original ideas is to utilize the NGT (Delbecq, Van de Ven, & Gustafson, 1975). Benefits of using the NGT are that all group members contribute in the exchange of ideas, all ideas are listed and considered, and through maximum participation the pool of possibilities is expanded.

Strategy: Consultees were grouped together according to their school levels and/or school responsibility (e.g., all elementary teachers, all elementary counselors, all middle school teachers, all administrators, etc.). Each group brainstormed how their particular group could be more invitational with students and parents. Five minutes was allotted for each person in the group to brainstorm individually and silently write their responses on note cards. Then in round-robin fashion, each person in the small group offered one suggestion (which was recorded on newsprint) until all ideas were listed. At the conclusion of the activity, each group reported their ideas to the larger group. When the groups reported, they were asked to omit any ideas that had been previously named by other groups. As a reference for the next and final activity of the in-service, all group suggestions were posted around the room.

<u>Problem Identification and Problem-Solving: Prioritizing and Changing</u>. The final in-service activity brought the school teams together to have them experience the last two steps of the group development model. We stressed to the consultees that the teams would experience these steps in an abbreviated fashion.

Intent: The brainstorming activity is linked to problem identification as consultees discuss, clarify, and evaluate the strengths and limitations of the ideas previously generated. Consultees need to discuss ideas in a positive manner, avoiding making value judgments and derogatory remarks. It is the role of the consultant to keep the discussion moving, to keep the groups focused on the assigned task, and to help the groups define problems in specific and concrete terms. Problem solving is the final step of this group development model. The preceding steps have systematically built a spirit of teamwork, with the consultees empowered and ready to respond to the question "What CAN we do?" The consultees now move to develop a realistic plan to solve problems.

Strategy: As the final activity, the school teams were asked to select three ideas from the brainstorming lists that they felt could realistically be implemented in their school. The teams then listed those conditions that would facilitate and inhibit the implementation of these ideas in their schools. The last charge to the teams included recommended actions that would sustain the facilitative conditions and would reduce or eliminate the inhibiting conditions.

Closing: Taking it Back Home. The last thirty minutes of the in-service was a closing activity. Each consultee was asked to write a personal goal for addressing the needs of at-risk students and to have another consultee witness the goal statement. Consultees were encouraged to take their goal statements back to their schools and share their goals and progress as a model in their own in-service. Lastly, each consultee was asked to sum up his/her experience during the in-service with one word and share that word with the group. We thanked the consultees for their enthusiasm, willingness, genuineness, and creativity. We wished them well and ended with a poem. The project director made closing remarks, distributed the evaluation instruments, and issued the certificates of attendance and forms for continuing education credit. Our in-service was over; it was now up to our consultees to conduct theirs.

Disengagement. We engaged in formative evaluation as we progressed through the consultation stages. As we moved through

66

the entry and diagnosis stages, we continued to check with the project director, to keep him apprised of our progress, and to hear what was happening with his responsibilities for the in-service. We continued to engage in formative evaluation during the implementation of the in-service. We periodically checked with one another as the consultees were engaged in group activities to gauge how the process was going. We evaluated the first day's events and pinpointed several small concerns that we tried to modify the following day. We also assessed the second day with the project director immediately after the in-service ended.

We designed the evaluation instrument based on the goals and objectives that constituted the in-service. Based on the outcomes of the evaluations, the majority of the consultees were in agreement that the goals of the in-service were met. While the evaluation results remained with the project director as part of the evaluation materials for the project, we received a brief summary of the results and comments sections. One mistake that we made was in not requesting our own copies of all of the evaluation results.

We had no planned follow-up contact with the project director. He did not suggest one, and neither did we. This was probably the biggest weakness of this consultation experience. We would suggest scheduling a postconsultation follow-up if only to satisfy one's own sense of incompleteness. Although we saw the director and some of the consultees informally afterwards, we heard only incidentally about the long-range outcomes of our in-service. For us, disengagement and termination in educational and training consultation may be one of the most frustrating elements of this type of consultation. We find it disconcerting to leave and have no continuing responsibility or role once the contract for the consultation has been fulfilled.

Implications for Practice

Educational and training consultation is by its nature a contracted, specific, time-limited intervention. Therefore, whatever constitutes the education and training, whether it be an in-service, workshop, or presentation, planning is a critical element. If consultees are to benefit from the experience and feel their time has been well-served, the consultant must do her/his homework. In planning educational and training consultation, the generic model provides a very clear and thorough framework for planning and designing a systematic, organized approach to consultation.

The importance of formative evaluation cannot be overlooked. Formative evaluation allows consultants to "stay on track" with important elements in the planning and execution of the consultation. For example, by not having a planned postconsultation session, we were left without a feeling of complete closure. Perhaps, we would have been able to offer further assistance in helping the school system if we had asked for the postconsultation meeting. Had we focused more on the disengagement phases, we would have avoided this significant omission and would have considered more closely how disengagement is a process that requires planning too.

Another implication for effective practice that our case brings home is the importance of acknowledging the professionalism and expertise that adult learners bring as consultees. When we work in schools, we believe it is presumptuous and demeaning to ignore the background, knowledge and training of persons who work with students and parents on a daily basis. We appreciate that school personnel resent the ivory tower expert approach of some consultants. We have had the opportunity to consult with a number of school systems on such topics as conferencing with parents, creating positive school environments, establishing school counseling programs, and training in communication skills. We have typically been well-received, and we attribute that to our

68

regard and respect for the knowledge base of our consultees. We consult more as facilitators than as experts when working in schools. We believe it is important to create an environment in which school personnel, as consultees, feel empowered, encouraged, validated, and supported for what they know. We invite them to share their expertise with one another and with us. We believe that helping school personnel reach out and support one another is perhaps one of the most important contributions we can make as consultants in an educational setting.

Lastly, we believe that as consultants we must model what we are teaching and training others to do. In this way, we demonstrate our trust in ourselves and in what we are presenting. When appropriate, we participate in activities with the consultees. We do not ask others to engage in risks that we are not willing to take ourselves. We believe that the best way to encourage others to embrace our ideas, our theories, and our training models is by example.

References and Suggested Readings

Brown, D., Kurpius, D. J., & Morris, J. R. (1988). Handbook of consultation with individuals and small groups. Alexandria, VA: American Counseling Association.

Canfield, J., & Wells, H. C. (1976). 100 ways to enhance self-concept in the classroom: A handbook for teachers and parents. Englewood Cliffs, NJ: Prentice Hall.

Cuban, L. (1989). At-risk students: What teachers and principals can do. Educational Leadership, 46 (5), 29-32.

Clemes, H., & Bean, R. (1980). How to raise children's self-esteem. Los Angeles: Enrich/Price Stern Sloan.

Delbecq, A. L., Van de Ven, A. H., & Gustafson, D. H. (1975). Group techniques for program planning: A guide to nominal group and delphi techniques. Glenview, IL: Scott, Foresman.

Dougherty, A.M. (1995). Consultation: Practice and perspectives in school and community settings. (2nd Ed.). Pacific Grove, CA: Brooks/Cole. (Chapter 9).

Fine, M. (1988). Of kitsch and caring: The illusion of students-at-risk. The School Administrator, 45 (8), 16-18, 23.

Hamachek, D. (1987). Encounters with the self (3rd ed.). New York: Holt, Rinehart and Winston Co.

Hamby, J. V. (1989). How to get an "A" on your dropout prevention report card. Educational Leadership, 46 (5), 21-28.

Merritt, R. E., & Walley, D. D. (1977). The group leader's handbook: Resources, techniques, and survival skills. Champaign, IL: Research Press.

Myrick, R. (1993). Development guidance and counseling: A practical approach. (2nd ed.). Minneapolis, MN: Educational Media Corporation.

Peck, N., Law, A., & Mills, R. (1987). Dropout prevention: What we have learned. Ann Arbor, MI: ERIC/CAPS.

Purkey, W. & Novak, J. (1984). Inviting school success: A self-concept approach to teaching and learning. (2nd ed.). Belmont, CA: Wadsworth.

Slavin, R.E., & Madden, N. A. (1989). What works for students at risk: A research synthesis. Educational Leadership, 46 (5), 4-13.

Witmer, J. (1992). Valuing diversity and similarity: Bridging the gap through interpersonal skills. Minneapolis, MN: Educational Media Corporation.

Editor's Note: Now that you have read this case, reflect upon it and develop a list of five things you might have done differently if you were a consultant involved with this case.

CHAPTER FIVE

BEHAVIORAL CASE CONSULTATION WITH A TEACHER

Pamela Carrington Rotto

Setting and Background Issues

<u>Setting</u>. While working as a school psychologist in a suburban elementary school, I was contacted for assistance by Mrs. Smith, a third grade teacher, regarding the deficient academic performance and problematic behaviors of one of her students. Michael, an 8-year-old child, was one of 23 students in Mrs. Smith's classroom. Mrs. Smith was seeking help with Michael due to a number of concerns including poor classroom participation, difficulty initiating and completing assignments, failing to follow directions, and off-task behaviors which occasionally were disruptive within the classroom setting.

The elementary school in which this consultation took place had an enrollment of approximately 600 students in kindergarten through fifth grade. It was one of three elementary schools in a district serving approximately 3,000 students. The combined racial and

71

ethnic make-up of the student population in this particular school building was 11 percent. Approximately 38 percent of the student population qualified for the free or reduced lunch program. Along with a full-time school counselor, I provided support services 3 days weekly at this school.

Background. Michael lived with his birth parents and 5-year-old brother. His father and mother had attained bachelor's degrees and were employed professionally in the community. According to his mother, Michael's developmental and medical histories were unremarkable. He was diagnosed with allergies which were managed using antihistamines.

Review of Michael's school records revealed a history of difficulties which dated to the first grade with work completion, poor motivation, and following directions. His former teachers described Michael as a child who required significant adult attention in the classroom to address his inappropriate behaviors and lack of work production. However, Michael's teachers also noted that he displayed creativity and interest in specific, nonacademic subject areas (e.g., boxing, karate, baseball). Michael previously had been evaluated for special education services but was determined ineligible. Results of intellectual assessment indicated average abilities. Michael's parents historically had been supportive of school-based interventions to address his academic and behavioral difficulties and had been involved in regular communication with Michael's teachers.

Prior to consultation services, Mrs. Smith had initiated several strategies, with the cooperation of Michael's parents, in an effort to decrease his problematic classroom behaviors and to improve his work habits. For example, Mrs. Smith increased the frequency of home-school communication by notifying Michael's parents of his problematic behaviors at school and urging them to provide consequences for these behaviors at home. She also offered Michael a weekly reward of free time for good behavior and timely completion of all classroom assignments. Incomplete assignments were sent home for completion. Michael also was given a daily assignment sheet and required to record assignments from each subject area and obtain the signature of his parents indicating that his work had been completed at home.

These strategies were judged ineffective by Michael's teacher and parents for several reasons and were gradually discontinued. Michael never earned the free time his teacher had offered. He frequently failed to bring his assignment sheet and school materials home; therefore, his mother would drive him back to school almost daily to retrieve the needed materials. Michael's parents quickly became frustrated by the burden of assisting him in transporting his materials to and from school, providing consequences at home for inappropriate school behaviors, and working for lengthy periods of time each evening to ensure that Michael completed his homework. Michael's resistance and refusal to begin and/or complete his homework in a timely manner were highly disruptive at home and negatively impacted family interactions. Mrs. Smith eventually stopped giving Michael homework because it rarely was completed.

Consultation Goals

Behavioral case consultation provided a direct link between assessment and treatment activities in response to this teacher's request for functional and effective classroom-based services. This systematic form of service delivery in which two persons work together to identify, analyze, remediate, and evaluate a client's needs has been recognized widely for its features of indirect service delivery and collaborative problem-solving. Two primary goals traditionally have been associated with behavioral consultation services:

a.   to provide a method for changing a child's behavioral, academic, or social problems, and

b.   to improve the consultee's skills so that she or he can prevent or respond effectively to future problems as well as to similar problems in other children (Bergan & Kratochwill, 1990; Kratochwill & Bergan, 1990).

Whereas the above goals of consultation defined the desired service outcomes overall, specific objectives were met and various strategies were used during each stage of consultation to facilitate accurate problem specification and effective problem resolution. The process of behavioral consultation has been characterized by the four stages of problem identification, problem analysis, plan implementation, and plan evaluation (Bergan & Kratochwill, 1990; Kratochwill & Bergan, 1990). These stages provided structure and focus to the problem-solving interaction and paralleled the generic consultation process of entry, diagnosis, implementation, and disengagement (Dougherty, 1995). With the exception of the plan implementation phase, these identified stages of behavioral consultation were procedurally operationalized through three interviews which tended to overlap in a dynamic, reciprocal fashion. The interested reader is referred to the companion resources of Bergan and Kratochwill (1990), and Kratochwill and Bergan (1990), as well as Kratochwill, Elliott, and Carrington Rotto (in press) for detailed outlines and comprehensive descriptions of the major components of behavioral consultation.

During the first stage of consultation, problem identification, my primary goal was to specify Michael's problem behaviors in clear, objective terms. The principal goal during the second problem analysis stage was to link the assessment data directly to a treatment plan. The treatment implementation stage followed clear identification and specification of the target behavior, systematic analysis of the baseline assessment data, verification of the nature of Michael's difficulty, and agreement on a treatment plan. The primary goal during this stage of behavioral consultation was implementation of a systematic plan by the teacher. The fourth stage of <u>treatment evaluation</u> was accompanied by the consultation goals of evaluating treatment effectiveness and programming for generalization and maintenance (Bergan & Kratochwill, 1990; Kratochwill & Bergan, 1990).

Consultant Function and Role

Behavioral consultation involves a collaborative relationship in which the consultant functions as a facilitator and coordinator. As such, behavioral consultants require knowledge and competence in at least three broad areas:

a. the process of consultative problem-solving (i.e., procedural knowledge of the stages and objectives of behavioral consultation);
b. the content of consultation interactions (i.e., knowledge regarding assessment, intervention, child development and learning processes, and child or population specific considerations), and
c. the dimensions of the consultation relationship.

Although consultant competence in coordinating the problem-solving process and generating behavior change methods are necessary conditions of behavioral consultation, they are not sufficient to facilitate effective consultation interactions. Integration of positive interpersonal skills and understanding with technical expertise are equally important to maximize consultant-consultee effectiveness (Sheridan, Salmon, Kratochwill, & Carrington Rotto, 1992).

During the present consultation case, I conceptualized my role as consultant using this framework of procedural and content knowledge and relationship considerations. My role as consultant was enhanced by procedural knowledge of the stages and objectives of behavioral consultation which was used to elicit a description of the problem, assist in analyzing the problem, devise a plan for intervention, and monitor the program once implemented. Knowledge and expertise regarding child and population considerations were applied to assess broad dimensions of the problem accurately, identify potentially important intervening variables, generate and examine case-related hypotheses, identify factors that could impact problem solution, and develop an appropriate as well as effective intervention. Basic interpersonal and communication skills, including sensitivity to issues of importance to the teacher, were essential at every stage of consultation to develop a positive consulting relationship and to facilitate movement toward problem management. This interpersonal relationship played a major role in the use and effectiveness of behavioral consultation. Issues of trust, genuineness, and openness were important qualities within the relationship, particularly due to the predominant use of an interview mode of information gathering and sharing (Conoley & Conoley, 1992; Martin, 1978). Thus, personal characteristics, professional competencies, and behavioral principles of reinforcement and modeling all were important elements in establishing and maintaining constructive and professional interactions.

Consultee's Experience in Consultation

The consultee, Mrs. Smith, had no prior experience with the behavioral consultation model. During three years of teaching the third grade, Mrs. Smith typically had requested direct psychological services such as assessment and counseling in response to academic and behavioral difficulties displayed by students in her classroom. This pattern of referral was consistent with observations of the substantial variability among teachers in their use of consultation and their significantly greater frequency

76

of requests for direct psychological services than for consultative assistance from the school psychologist (Bardon, 1982; Piersel & Gutkin, 1983).

Studies investigating actual participation in consultation have revealed that less experienced teachers are more likely to use this method of service delivery (Gutkin & Bossard, 1984) and that teachers prefer consultation for less severe problems (Gutkin, Singer, & Brown, 1980) and for problems over which they perceive themselves to have a relatively high degree of control (Gutkin & Ajchenbaum, 1984). In addition, teachers seek consultation for behavioral problems more frequently than for academic problems (Hughes, Grossman, & Barker, 1990).

Since Mrs. Smith had no prior experience in behavioral consultation, time was spent overviewing this model of service delivery and explaining what might be accomplished through consultation. We also discussed her role as consultee which was defined as providing a clear description of the problem, working with Michael to implement the intervention program, observing progress, periodically evaluating the plan's effectiveness, and supervising Michael's actions (Elliott & Sheridan, 1992). Discussion of these issues at the time of referral also provided an opportunity to inquire and gain preliminary insight into important classroom systems variables such as physical and environmental factors, academic and curricular issues, behavior management strategies, child and family characteristics, and the relationship between home and school. Since systems variables may at times transcend individual variables, it was important for me to understand the realities of the classroom in order to better understand the individuals within that setting (Conoley & Conoley, 1992).

Application: Consultant Techniques and Procedures

Entry. The problem identification stage involved specifying and defining the problems to be targeted in consultation. My primary objective during this stage was to attain clarification of the referral concern which then would lead to designation of the goals to be achieved through consultation, measurement of current child performance with respect to these goals, and assessment of the discrepancy between current and desired performance. This sequence of problem-solving activities involved identification of

      a.   target behaviors,
      b.   problem frequency, duration, and intensity,
      c.   conditions under which the target behaviors occurred,
      d   the required level of performance,
      e.   the student's strengths,
      f.   behavioral assessment procedures, and
      g.   consultee effectiveness (Bergan & Kratochwill, 1990; Kratochwill & Bergan, 1990; Witt & Elliott, 1983).

A variety of assessment strategies (i.e., teacher rating scale, behavioral interviews, and direct observations) were used during the problem identification stage to obtain a comprehensive evaluation of Michael's problematic behaviors. These strategies provided continuous opportunities to refine specification of the target behaviors, identify salient factors and conditions surrounding the occurrence of these behaviors, and test hypotheses regarding potential factors that may have enhanced or impeded intervention implementation and effectiveness.

Completion of the Teacher Report Form (Achenbach & Edelbrock, 1986) by Mrs. Smith provided broad assessment of problem behaviors and objective data regarding the severity of these behaviors relative to a standardized population. This measure is a multidimensional scale designed to record behavioral problems of children between the ages of 4 and 16. It also provides useful information regarding global changes in child behaviors and covariational effects (i.e., generalization to collateral behaviors). Results from this teacher rating scale yielded clinically significant T-scores on the uncommunicative, hyperactive, aggressive, and delinquent subscales.

Mrs. Smith's concerns were described and defined in detail during the Problem Identification Interview (PII). She identified problems such as Michael's poor participation, difficulty initiating and completing assignments, failure to follow directions, and disorganized and off-task behaviors. Two primary areas of difficulty emerged as Mrs. Smith detailed her observations and impressions of Michael. First, Mrs. Smith described deficits in Michael's academic performance. At this point, it was important to determine whether Michael's academic difficulties resulted primarily from performance deficits or from skill deficits (Elliott & Shapiro, 1990). Therefore, classroom work samples and results of past testing were reviewed, revealing that the problems and questions Michael completed generally were accurate and documenting acquisition of the skills necessary to perform grade-level work. Review of classroom progress to date indicated that while Michael's assignment completion difficulties were pervasive across subject areas, he demonstrated an inconsistent performance pattern within each academic subject. Thus, Michael's academic difficulties appeared to be the result of performance deficits rather than skill deficits.

Mrs. Smith also described concerns regarding Michael's demonstration of problematic behaviors at school. Further discussion suggested that many of these behaviors likely were related to failures in task accuracy and completion (e.g., off-task behaviors, daydreaming, distractibility). As it became clear that Mrs. Smith's primary concerns were related to Michael's work production difficulties, this area was targeted for intervention.

79

Work completion also was selected as a target area because its occurrence was incompatible with Michael's other problematic behaviors. It was anticipated that improvement in Michael's work production might be accompanied by collateral improvement in his inappropriate behaviors.

Mrs. Smith estimated that Michael typically completed less than 40 percent of his classroom assignments when given individual attention and frequent reminders to remain on task. Without prompts, his daily average productivity decreased to less than 20 percent. Although Mrs. Smith reported that Michael's daily productivity was problematic across subject areas, it was decided that a single subject (i.e., mathematics) would be targeted first for treatment purposes. Work completion initially was operationally defined as completing assignments during classroom time, following directions, and coming to class with the appropriate materials (e.g., book, paper, and pencil). Later, this operational definition was revised to include four behavioral components (i.e., materials ready, start working immediately, work until the job is finished, and place completed work in the assignment basket).

During the problem identification stage, it was important to determine how much Michael actually was working compared to his teacher's expectations. At first, it seemed desirable for Michael to work nonstop for the entire academic subject period. However, this expectation later was believed to be both unrealistic and unnecessary. Mrs. Smith indicated that it would be acceptable for Michael to work at a pace similar to that of another student who worked at a reasonable rate. It was decided that data would be collected to determine how long it took another student of average ability to finish an identical assignment with subsequent comparison of Michael's performance to this time estimate.

Mrs. Smith kept track of both students' performance in the selected subject area of mathematics for one week. Teacher prompts and individual attention were not provided for either student during this time. Data indicated that Michael's performance varied, with 20 percent assignment completion during the time it took the other student to finish the math assignment on the first day. On the remaining days, Michael completed 40 percent, 10 percent, 25 percent and 0 percent of the assignments, while the comparison student finished each assignment. Overall, Michael completed 19 percent of the math assignments for the week during the classroom work period. On one of the days, Mrs. Smith noted that Michael seemed to work slightly faster when he noticed the teacher keeping track of his progress. However, he did not maintain this increase in production consistently across days.

Diagnosis. During the problem analysis stage of consultation, we focused on further exploration of the problem through the evaluation of baseline data, identification of variables that might contribute to problem solution, and development of a specific plan to implement during the treatment stage. The process of problem analysis was completed in two phases. First, we identified factors that might influence the attainment of a solution to the identified problem (i.e., the analysis phase). Second, we used these factors in the design of a plan to solve the problem (i.e., the plan design phase). Specific steps included

    a.   evaluating the initial assessment data,
    b.   conducting a functional analysis of conditions that may impact the target behavior,
    c.   further identifying the nature of the target behavior,
    d.   developing plan strategies and tactics, and
    e.   establishing procedures to assess performance during plan implementation (Bergan & Kratochwill, 1990; Kratochwill & Bergan, 1990).

The procedures of problem analysis were instituted via the Problem Analysis Interview (PAI).

Following completion of the PII, two weeks elapsed before Mrs. Smith and I were able to schedule a second meeting. Mrs. Smith continued to collect baseline data on the rate and accuracy of Michael's math assignment completion during this time, although she did not document the rate of assignment completion for the comparison student. The baseline data initially collected on Michael and his classmate indicated that the other student had successfully completed each of his assignments in the allotted time. Mrs. Smith believed that math was easier for Michael and that he should be able to complete his assignments within a similar time frame. However, baseline data revealed that Michael's performance continued to vary, with an overall rate of 19 percent completion during the second week and 14 percent completion during the third week. As we reviewed the available assessment data during the PAI, we developed a more complete problem formulation which included etiological factors as well as the influence of ecological factors in the development and maintenance of the problem.

Time during the problem analysis also was devoted to generating alternative strategies for resolving the problem, selecting strategies for implementation, and planning the implementation steps. The goal of consultation was to devise a plan to increase Michael's academic production (with an initial focus on completion of math assignments). However, it was difficult to determine what factors might motivate him to work more diligently. Since it was important to identify desirable reinforcers, a reinforcement survey was provided. While administering this questionnaire to Michael, Mrs. Smith discussed her concerns regarding his assignment completion as well as some of his responses to the survey. Following this interaction, Mrs. Smith noted that Michael seemed to enjoy the individual attention he had received from her. Survey results revealed interests in activities such as board games, Nintendo, reading books, baseball cards, basketball, playing with favorite toys, and making and fixing things. As we completed the objectives of the problem analysis stage, a three-fold plan was

82

devised to help Michael accomplish the goal of increasing his work production. This treatment plan is described below in the implementation section.

Since one of the main objectives of problem analysis was to develop an intervention to address the identified problem, it was important to obtain information regarding the preferences of the treatment agent (i.e., Mrs. Smith) to facilitate development of a feasible and manageable plan. Mrs. Smith's perceptions and opinions regarding the treatment procedures were critical in that implementation of the program likely would be impacted by whether she found the procedures practical, feasible, and otherwise acceptable. A number of factors have been found to impact a teacher's acceptability of an intervention. These include time required to implement the intervention, risk to the target child, potential side effects for other non-target students, and perceived fairness (Elliott, 1988a; Kazdin, 1981). Therefore, treatment acceptability was assessed during the PAI using interviewing strategies. However, a number of rating scales have been developed for formal, data-based assessment of pre-treatment acceptability, and readers are encouraged to consult this material (Elliott, 1988b; Witt & Elliott, 1985).

Implementation. Treatment implementation involved the introduction of the plan, or treatment program, which had been designed during the problem analysis stage. Although there was no formal interview during this stage, the goal of consultation at this point was to maximize the likelihood that the plan would result in desired outcomes. For this reason, it was important to attend to the three major tasks of plan implementation which included facilitating skill development of the consultee (if necessary), monitoring the implementation process, and assisting with plan revisions. Likewise, procedural details such as assigning specific individuals to various roles and gathering or preparing materials were essential (Bergan & Kratochwill, 1990; Kratochwill & Bergan, 1990).

The treatment plan consisted of three components. First, a chart which contained a box for every day of the week was placed on Michael's desk. Michael could earn up to two stars in each box daily. At the beginning of each math period, the number of problems on the daily assignment was divided by two. The resulting figure was the number of problems Michael had to earn during each half of the math period to earn a star. For example, if the math assignment consisted of 24 problems on Monday and the period was 40 minutes long, Michael would need to complete 12 problems in the first 20 minutes to receive one star. Similarly, he would need to complete 12 problems during the second 20 minutes to earn a second star. Each half of the period was independent of the other so that even if Michael failed to earn the first star, he still could earn a star during the second half of the time period. Dividing the assignments in half allowed Michael to receive reinforcement and feedback regarding his progress at briefer intervals. It also may have served to make the assignments appear less formidable.

The second part of the plan involved long term reinforcement for weekly attainment of a target number of stars. Because Michael seemed to value individualized attention from his teacher, it seemed likely that he would be motivated to work for this reinforcement, particularly when it involved desirable activities. However, it was neither feasible nor practical for Mrs. Smith to set aside a block of time to spend with Michael each week. Since Michael had expressed an interest in "making and fixing things," the school custodian was approached, and he subsequently agreed to allow Michael to accompany and assist him for 30 minutes each Friday following successful attainment of the target number of stars.

The third component of the plan consisted of Mrs. Smith meeting with Michael and his parents prior to implementation to discuss the intervention. The primary purpose of this strategy was to promote more positive home-school communication, since prior contacts between Mrs. Smith and Michael's parents had become increasingly focused on his negative behaviors at school. In addition, Mrs. Smith wanted to involve Michael and to encourage him to accept appropriate ownership for the plan, which was considered critical for his success. During this meeting, Michael's parents expressed frustration regarding previous school expectations that they address and provide consequences for Michael's negative school behaviors. It was decided that Michael's parents would be involved in the positive aspects of his treatment program. More specifically, information regarding Michael's success would be communicated to his parents regularly via a "note home" system so that they could reward progress instead of providing consequences for deficiencies. In addition, Michael no longer would be expected to take his incomplete assignments home for completion, although he would continue to receive routine homework assignments which were consistent with those of his classmates (e.g., studying for spelling tests, social studies and science projects).

Since Mrs. Smith clearly demonstrated the skills and competencies necessary for plan implementation, it was not necessary to provide additional training to develop important skills for executing the treatment plan. As Mrs. Smith implemented the program, I continued to maintain contact with her for purposes of monitoring the implementation process, assisting in plan revision, and scheduling subsequent meetings. Monitoring plan implementation was completed in two ways. First, Mrs. Smith maintained an ongoing record of Michael's progress (i.e., production and accuracy). This monitoring was a continuation of the problem identification and problem analysis phases of consultation and remained consistent with baseline data collection procedures. A second type of monitoring activity involved evaluation of the strategies associated with the treatment plan. Together Mrs. Smith and I monitored plan implementation and integrity by discussing the intervention plan periodically. This strategy was complemented by occasional classroom observations which provided an opportunity for me to observe child and consultee behaviors and to determine the need for revisions in the plan. Another method for monitoring treatment integrity which was not used in the present case, involves asking the consultee to report integrity data periodically (Gresham, 1989).

While the basic components of the plan remained consistent, the target number of stars needed for weekly reinforcement activities gradually was increased. Significant changes in the plan were not necessary in the present case because Michael's behavior was changing in the desired direction. However, if this outcome had not occurred, it would have been necessary to make changes in the plan. It may have become necessary to return to the problem analysis phase to further analyze variables such as the setting, intrapersonal child characteristics, or skill deficits; or to the problem identification stage to determine whether the nature of the problem had changed.

Disengagement. Finally, treatment evaluation was undertaken to determine the extent to which the intervention plan was successful. Primary goals during this stage included assessing goal attainment, evaluating treatment effectiveness, and post-implementation planning. Treatment evaluation was essential to the process of behavioral consultation at this point because it facilitated a mutual decision regarding whether consultation should be continued or terminated, and whether a post-implementation plan should be initiated to facilitate generalization and maintenance of the desired behavior (Bergan & Kratochwill, 1990; Kratochwill & Bergan, 1990).

The treatment evaluation phase was instituted following 5 weeks of program implementation. During the Treatment Evaluation Interview (TEI), Mrs. Smith and I discussed issues surrounding attainment of the consultation goals, effectiveness of the intervention plan, and acceptability of the treatment to both her and Michael. The process of evaluating goal attainment and treatment effectiveness was accomplished using information from a variety of sources including direct observations, behavioral interviews, rating scales, and social validation. Single subject design also facilitated determination of whether a functional relationship existed between the specific intervention strategy and the resulting behavior change. It also provided an evaluation of the need for modification, continuation, or termination of treatment (Barlow, Hayes, & Nelson, 1984).

Results from direct observations of Michael's daily output are presented in Figure 1. Data indicated that Michael completed an average of 75 percent of his assignments while the plan was in effect. Likewise, Michael earned enough stars to receive his weekly reinforcement 4 out of 5 weeks (i.e., all but Week 3). This increase in Michael's assignment production was significant, relative to his completion rate demonstrated during baseline data collection. A decrease in productivity was observed during Week 2 of treatment and may have reflected the presence of a substitute teacher in the classroom at the beginning of the week. It is not unusual to observe variability in client performance during implementation of a new program, and a substitute teacher may have exacerbated this variability.

Figure 1 - Percentage of Math Assignments Completed Daily

Day	Percentage Completed	Phase
1	20	Baseline
2	40	
3	10	
4	25	
5	0	

Day	Percentage Completed	Phase
6	30	
7	10	
8	25	
9	20	
10	10	
11	0	
12	0	
13	35	
14	15	
15	20	
16	60	Treatment
17	75	
18	55	
19	65	
20	100	
21	85	
22	70	
23	65	
24	90	
25	85	
26	50	
27	45	
28	50	
29	60	
30	30	
31	75	
32	80	
33	100	
34	95	
35	90	

Day	Percentage Completed	Phase
36	100	
37	100	
38	80	
39	75	
40	90	

Social validation criteria also were used to determine whether the intervention program had brought Michael's performance within the range of acceptable behavior as compared to a typical peer of average ability. Mrs. Smith collected data on the rate of work production and level of accuracy of the identified comparison peer during the last week of the program. Results indicated that while Michael's level of accuracy was comparable to that of his peer, his rate of production continued to be discrepant. However, Mrs. Smith noted that Michael's production rate had improved dramatically and was approaching more acceptable levels of performance.

Information gathered through post-treatment completion of a teacher rating scale and the TEI also revealed consistent findings. Results from the TRF documented improved behavior in the classroom. During the interview, Mrs. Smith stated that Michael's rate of work completion in math had improved significantly and that his behaviors were less problematic during this period. Informal assessment of the acceptability of treatment following implementation revealed that Mrs. Smith viewed the plan as an appropriate and reasonable method of addressing Michael's needs. However, she also expressed concern that Michael had not shown spontaneous improvement in his work production in other subject areas. This information was not surprising in light of the abundant evidence in the treatment literature that specific procedures are needed to facilitate generalization and maintenance of behavior. Although generalization may occur naturally, it typically must be programmed using strategies which may be put into place during the treatment evaluation phase of consultation. Since generalization did not occur in nontraining settings (i.e., other academic content areas), a decision was made to leave the present plan in effect to continue to modify and maintain Michael's improvements in math while expanding the program to address his difficulties in science. Thus, post-implementation planning focused on modifying the treatment plan, identifying strategies to facilitate generalization and maintenance, and devising a system for follow-up recording procedures to monitor Michael's progress over time. Given the continuing needs of this case, the consultation relationship was not terminated at this time. Rather, a mutual decision to conclude consultation followed attainment of the consultation goals which included generalization of behaviors and maintenance of treatment gains.

Implications for Practice

Traditionally, behavioral consultation has been implemented with classroom teachers in an effort to establish intervention programs in regular education and thereby reduce the number of placements in special education programs. However, school-based consultation services have been expanded to include work with special education teachers (Kratochwill, Sheridan, Carrington Rotto, & Salmon, 1991) and teachers of early intervention programs for preschool-age children (Kratochwill & Elliott, 1993) within the past decade. While initial efforts primarily targeted behavioral problems in children, behavioral consultation has been used increasingly to remediate academic and socialization difficulties in school settings. This emphasis on retention and direct intervention with teachers is reflected in the present case example which illustrates the use of behavioral consultation in the school setting to address the academic productivity of an underachieving student.

Behavioral consultation with teachers is an effective method of remediating school-based problems. However, this narrow focus often fails to address the broader context within which the child's problems may occur. Behavioral consultation recently has been expanded to include parents and teachers in a conjoint fashion in an effort to consider the broader behavioral interrelationships across environments and to serve as a link among the significant settings in a child's life (Sheridan & Kratochwill, 1992; Sheridan, Kratochwill, & Bergan, in press). Conjoint behavioral consultation, when conducted with parents and teachers, has been shown to provide a feasible, effective means of linking assessment to treatment in the provision of indirect services to socially withdrawn children (Sheridan, Kratochwill, & Elliott, 1990). In this model, parents and teachers jointly and actively serve as consultees, with an emphasis on interactions and collaboration between home and school systems. Strengths of this model include involvement of parents and teachers in a structured problem-solving framework, collection of comprehensive and systematic data across extended temporal and contextual bases, and consistent programming across settings to maximize treatment effects, allow for assessment of behavioral contrast or side effects, and enhance generalization and maintenance (Sheridan & Elliott, 1991).

Use of behavioral consultation also has been extended beyond the schools to address problematic child behaviors which are observed predominantly in the home and/or community settings but not in the school setting. Parent-only consultation has been used to enhance the effects of competency-based parent training in managing problematic behaviors in school-age children (Carrington Rotto & Kratochwill, in press) and has been advanced as a model of early intervention with the goal of decreasing noncompliant and aggressive behaviors in preschool-age children (Carrington Rotto & Kratochwill, 1993). Strengths of this model include parent involvement in a structured problem-solving framework, use of parent training methodology to teach parents specific skills which enhance plan implementation, and opportunities for early intervention services prior to school entry.

91

It is likely that the child and teacher outcomes from the present case example would have been enhanced by involving the parents and teacher in a conjoint behavioral consultation approach. Results from a recent study have suggested that conjoint behavioral consultation is an effective model of home-school collaboration in the remediation of academic performance deficits (Galloway & Sheridan, 1992). Although Michael's target behaviors improved in the school setting, these changes were not observed by his parents who continued to struggle to get Michael to complete homework assignments. To be truly effective, behaviors taught in any behavioral training program should generalize across time, settings, individuals, and behaviors. Thus, consideration of the use of conjoint behavioral consultation with Michael's teacher and parents would have been appropriate at the inception of this case.

An additional issue arose when Michael's parents later disclosed that they were struggling with significant management difficulties in response to their son's noncompliant and oppositional behaviors at home and in public. Michael's parents did not acknowledge their son's extensive behavioral difficulties until the later stages of treatment evaluation, and these problems were not addressed using the teacher-only model of behavioral consultation. In light of their apparent need for parenting support and skills training, later use of parent-only behavioral consultation in combination with parent training services also appeared appropriate for Michael's parents.

In sum, behavioral case consultation provides a useful problem-solving framework for working within and between family and school systems. This systematic model of indirect service delivery may be conducted with teachers, parents, or teacher-parent pairs to enhance child functioning across home, school, and community settings. Intervention plans may be developed and implemented to address diverse target problems in areas such as academic productivity, socialization, and behavioral difficulties. As research and practice in behavioral consultation continue to expand, it will be critical for consultants to attend closely to the diverse needs of various subject populations and to further examine alternative parent and teacher roles and levels of involvement in consultation.

References and Suggested Readings

Achenbach, T. M., & Edelbrock, C. S. (1986). Manual for the Teacher's Report Form and Teacher Version of the Child Behavior Profile. Burlington: University of Vermont, Department of Psychiatry.

Bardon, J. I. (1982). The psychology of school psychology. In C. R. Reynolds & T. B. Gutkin (Eds.), The handbook of school psychology (pp. 3-14). New York: Wiley.

Barlow, D. H., Hayes, S. C., & Nelson, R. O. (1984). The scientist-practitioner: Research and accountability in clinical and educational settings. New York: Pergamon Press.

Bergan, J. R., & Kratochwill, T. R. (1990). Behavioral consultation in applied settings. New York: Plenum Press.

Carrington Rotto, P., & Kratochwill, T. R. (in press). Behavioral consultation with parents: Using competency-based training to modify child noncompliance. School Psychology Review.

Carrington Rotto, P., & Kratochwill, T. R. (1993, April). Competency-based parent consultation and training to modify noncompliance in young children. Paper presented at the 25th Annual Meeting of the National Association of School Psychologists, Washington, D. C.

Conoley, J. C., & Conoley, C. W. (1992). School consultation: A guide to practice and training (2nd ed.). New York: Pergamon Press.

Dougherty, A. M. (1995). Consultation: Practice and Perspectives in School and Community Settings. (2nd ed.). Pacific Grove, CA: Brooks/Cole Publishing Company.

Elliott, S. N. (1988a). Acceptability of behavioral treatments:

Review of variables that influence treatment selection. Professional Psychology: Research and Practice, 19, 68-80.

Elliott, S. N. (1988b). Acceptability of behavioral treatment in educational settings. In J. C. Witt, S. N. Elliott, & F. M. Gresham (Eds.), The handbook of behavior therapy in education (pp. 121-150). New York: Plenum Publishers.

Elliott, S. N., & Shapiro, E. S. (1990). Intervention techniques and programs for academic performance problems. In T. B. Gutkin & C. R. Reynolds (Eds.), The handbook of school psychology (2nd ed.) (pp. 637-662). New York: Wiley.

Elliott, S. N., & Sheridan, S. M. (1992). Consultation conferencing: Problem-solving among educators, parents, and support personnel. Elementary School Journal, 92, 261-284.

Galloway, J., & Sheridan, S. M. (1992, March). Parent-teacher consultation: Forging effective home-school partnerships in the treatment of academic underachievement. Paper presented at the 24th Annual Meeting of the National Association of School Psychologists, Nashville.

Gresham, F. M. (1989). Assessment of treatment integrity in school consultation and prereferral intervention. School Psychology Review, 18, 37-50.

Gutkin, T. B., & Ajchenbaum, M. (1984). Teachers' perceptions of control and preferences for consultative services. Professional Psychology: Research and Practice, 15, 565-570.

Gutkin, T. B., & Bossard, M. D. (1984). The impact of consultant, consultee, and organizational variables on teacher attitudes toward consultation services. Journal of School Psychology, 22, 251-258.

Gutkin, T. B., Singer, J. H., & Brown, R. (1980). Teacher reactions to school-based consultation services: A multivariate analysis. Journal of School Psychology, 18, 125-134.

Hughes, J. N., Grossman, P., & Barker, D. (1990). Teachers' expectancies, participation in consultation, and perceptions of consultant helpfulness. School Psychology Quarterly, 5, 167-179.

Kazdin, A. E. (1981). Acceptability of child treatment techniques: The influence of treatment efficacy and adverse side effects. Behavior Therapy, 12, 493-506.

Kazdin, A. E. (1989). Behavior modification in applied settings (revised edition). Homewood, IL: Dorsey Press.

Kratochwill, T. R., & Bergan, J. R. (1990). Behavioral consultation in applied settings: An individual guide. New York: Plenum Press.

Kratochwill, T. R., & Elliott, S. N. (1993). An experimental analysis of teacher/parent mediated interventions for preschoolers with behavioral problems. Unpublished manuscript, Office of Special Education and Rehabilitative Services, U. S. Department of Education, Wisconsin Center for Education Research, University of Wisconsin-Madison, Madison, WI.

Kratochwill, T. R., Elliott, S. N., & Carrington Rotto, P. (in press). Best practices in school based behavioral consultation. In A. Thomas & J. Grimes (Eds.), Best practices in school psychology - III. Washington, D. C.: NASP.

Kratochwill, T. R., & Morris, R. J. (Eds.) (1992). The practice of child therapy (2nd ed.). Boston: Allyn & Bacon.

Kratochwill, T. R., Sheridan, S. M., Carrington Rotto, P., & Salmon D. (1991). Preparation of school psychologists to serve as consultants for teachers of emotionally disturbed children. School Psychology Review, 20, 530-550.

Martin, R. P. (1978). Expert and referent power: A framework for understanding and maximizing consultation effectiveness. Journal of School Psychology, 16, 49-55.

Piersel, W. C., & Gutkin, T. B. (1983). Resistance to school-based consultation: A behavioral analysis of the problem. Psychology in the Schools, 20, 311-320.

Sheridan, S. M., & Elliott, S. N. (1991). Behavioral consultation as a process for linking the assessment and treatment of social skills. Journal of Educational and Psychological Consultation, 2, 151-173.

Sheridan, S. M., & Kratochwill, T. R. (1992). Behavioral parent-teacher consultation: Conceptual and research considerations. Journal of School Psychology, 30, 117-139.

Sheridan, S. M., Kratochwill, T. R., & Bergan, J. (in press). Conjoint behavioral consultation: A procedural manual. New York: Plenum Press.

Sheridan, S. M., Kratochwill, T. R., & Elliott, S. N. (1990). Behavioral consultation with parents and teachers: Delivering treatment for socially withdrawn children at home and school. School Psychology Review, 19, 33-52.

Sheridan, S. M., Salmon, D., Kratochwill, T. R., & Carrington Rotto, P. (1992). A conceptual model for the expansion of behavioral consultation training. Journal of Educational and Psychological Consultation, 3, 193-218.

Witt, J. C., & Elliott, S. N. (1983). Assessment in behavioral consultation: The initial interview. School Psychology Review, 12, 42-49.

Witt, J. C., & Elliott, S. N. (1985). Acceptability of classroom intervention strategies. In T. R. Kratochwill (Ed.), Advances in school psychology (Vol. IV, pp. 251-288). Hillsdale, NJ: Lawrence Erlbaum Associates.

Zins, J. E., Kratochwill, T. R., & Elliott, S. N. (Eds.). (1993). Handbook of consultation services for children. San Francisco: Jossey-Bass.

Editor's Note: Now that you have read this case, reflect upon it and develop a list of five things you might have done differently if you were a consultant involved with the case.

CHAPTER SIX

GROUP CONSULTATION WITH

A UNIVERSITY COUNSELING CENTER STAFF

Frances E. Tack and A. Michael Dougherty

Setting and Background Issues

Setting. The consultation took place at the counseling center of a medium-sized university in a small southeastern college town. The counseling center employs four full-time professional counselors and provides internship opportunities for four students per semester. The center offers individual counseling, group counseling, and campus education seminars on a wide range of topics including multicultural sensitivity, stress management, and conflict resolution. Four years ago the center moved from a shared location on the lower floor of an administration building to a stand alone facility. This move provided additional confidentiality as well as more room in which to conduct workshops and group counseling. This move also included the addition of several more individual counseling rooms and group rooms equipped with

97

monitoring equipment for supervising interns (including two-way mirrors and microphones).

The center serves a total university student population of 8,000, about a quarter of whom seek services from the center annually. The university itself is a private university dedicated to offering a broad range of bachelor's, master's and doctoral level curricula, including courses of study in biology, psychology, education, chemistry and counseling. The students are generally academically focused and the graduation rate exceeds seventy percent. The school also boasts a strong varsity and intramural athletic program in which about half of all students participate.

Background. The consultation evolved due to staff interest in: 1) exploring avenues for acquiring funding to pay interns; and 2) learning more about the consultation process. For several years prior to the consultation, the director of the counseling center had worked with the staff to acquire funding for clinical graduate assistantships. The director met with little success, primarily due to the tight funding constraints of the university. Having talked with many people through the course of this investigation and receiving no commitment, the director decided to approach us to consult with them concerning the acquisition of funding for interns.

Concurrently, the staff recognized a need for additional training on the consultation process and agreed that the consultation about internship funding could also be used as training on the consultation process itself. Both of these goals were communicated to us when we were requested to conduct the consultation. This dual goal presented a great opportunity for us to spread the word about consultation within human services but at the same time added some additional complexity to the consultation process. Specifically, we recognized that we would need to plan an approach that would simultaneously produce an action plan related to the funding question and leave the participants more aware of and knowledgeable about the consultation process. This would all need to be accomplished in one day.

It was also communicated to us from the beginning that current counseling center interns would participate in the consultation. This issue forced us to be aware as we planned for the consultation that the interns would have limited knowledge on the institutional dynamics and the background of the problem. Therefore, we were aware of needing to incorporate these elements into the consultation.

Another element of interest is the fact that we had worked with the counseling center director and staff on numerous occasions in the past (though not in the role of consultants) and had a very positive working relationship already established. This fact helped to shorten the entry process since trust was already established and we had a wealth of background information on the center and its place within the larger institution. Our one concern in this area was the fact that one of the consultants was an administrator in a department which places interns at the counseling center and therefore had a potential conflict of interest. We discussed this with the director when the initial request for consultation was made. The director was not concerned about this fact and even suggested that it might be a benefit to the staff since we would have a "vested interest" in assisting them in acquiring funding. Though the director was not concerned, we kept this potential conflict in mind as we planned the consultation.

Consultation Goals

Going into the group consultation, we understood that the goals of the consultation were to assist the counseling center staff in defining the funding problem in finer detail, generating possible approaches, and learning more about the consultation process.

The group was interested in leaving the consultation with a list of specific avenues to pursue for funding of interns and an action plan including the what, who and when. Though the original goal was to pursue funding for interns, the discussion of goals during the actual group consultation led to an immediate consensus and the establishment of a broader goal, that of acquiring additional staff. This will be discussed in greater detail later in the case.

The consultees also wanted to leave the consultation with a general understanding of the skills and techniques of process consultation. To meet this goal, we envisioned a review of the stages of consultation and a discussion of selected techniques. We knew from the educational backgrounds of the staff that most of them had been exposed to teaching about consultation before; therefore, we did not plan to spend a lot of time *formally* teaching consultation. Instead we planned to conduct the consultation and then use it as a case example to review the basics of consultation and important issues that emerged.

Consultant Function and Roles

Driven by the dual goals of exploring the funding issue and learning about consultation, this consultation became a hybrid of process consultation and education/training consultation. This situation generated a subsequent hybrid of roles for us, including fact finders, process specialists, facilitators, collaborators and educators/trainers.

The role of fact finder occurred for us primarily during the initial meeting with the director. During this time we used an interview approach to learn about the background of the case and work that the director had done up to this point. This activity not only helped us to better understand the case but also provided an encapsulation for the director. As a result, the director used our fact finding discussion as the basis for development of a timeline that documented past attempts to acquire funding. This description included which organizations within the university had been approached, who specifically had been contacted, a summary of what had been discussed, and the results of the request. (This timeline was later used in the group consultation.)

In the roles of process specialists and facilitators, we acted as catalysts for group discussion, summarized input and made connections, and facilitated the brainstorming process. The resulting content was important. But, as process facilitators, our primary focus was on the process itself; namely, engaging all staff members in the dialogue, recording input, and working toward the development of an action plan.

In the role of collaborators, we provided input to the group on our own experiences in working to achieve funding for interns and our understanding of the system in which their pursuits were taking place. We shared a specific attempt we had made three years ago to fund an additional graduate assistant. We shared the names of persons we had contacted as well as our lack of success in getting what we had requested. This sharing produced mixed results from the group. On one hand, the group seemed validated that they were not the only ones not able to achieve additional funding for interns. However, the group also appeared somewhat frustrated by our experience in that, added to their own experience, additional funding was beginning to seem like an impossibility. This presented us as consultants with the challenge of keeping the group positive and focused on "possibility thinking" as they had requested. We did this by: 1) validating the frustration of the group; 2) sharing that we, too, had been frustrated at times; and 3) reframing the concerns by reminding them that there were still many options open which we and they had not yet tried.

As trainers, we discussed with the group the consultative techniques we used and how we had experienced the unfolding of the consultation. We shared where we thought transitions from one stage to another had occurred and the specific elements of each stage that we had attained. Further, we reviewed the brainstorming process and facilitation techniques in general, giving examples directly from the funding case we had just completed. We also facilitated their discussion of their perceptions of the consultation process in general. This helped us to understand areas that needed further elaboration as well as provided useful feedback for our own professional development as consultants.

Consultees' Experience in Consultation

During the consultation, the consultees brainstormed possible options for funding. They openly discussed their needs and concerns, and processed with each other various options. In this way, the consultees acted as problem solvers and collaborators with the consultants. The most significant aspect of the consultees' participation was in generating the action plan. As previously noted, in this phase the consultants were focused on the process and on extracting ideas from the consultees. The consultees provided the actual content as they brainstormed avenues for acquiring additional funding and staffing.

Another significant part of the experience for the consultees was receiving education/training on the consultation process. Since the format for this training was discussion of the case they had just participated in, the consultees played a dynamic part in their own exploration of the consultation process. They heard from the consultants and engaged in dialogue about various elements. In addition, they added input from their own past educational experiences in consultation and as consultees. This added a greater depth and variety to the discussion and allowed the consultees to not only learn from the consultants but also to learn from each other.

At the end of the consultation, we facilitated a discussion in which the entire group processed the consultation experience. During this time, the consultees indicated that the process had helped them to "get out of the box" in their thinking to generate options which before had not even occurred to them. They felt that the group format had allowed them to "play off each other" in generating ideas and that having an objective third party to facilitate had allowed all of the staff to participate more fully.

Application: Consultant Techniques and Procedures

Entry. The request for us to consult with the counseling center came originally from one of the staff counselors in a memo. In this memo, the counselor explained the dual needs the staff had of exploring intern funding options and learning more about the consultation process. She also explained the staff's interest in conducting the consultation as a group, including participation of the center's interns.

In our follow-up discussion with the staff member, we expressed our interest in learning more about the center's needs relative to the consultation, and we suggested a preliminary group meeting to help us better understand these needs. The staff member discussed this with the rest of the center's staff, and they decided that they were comfortable with just the center's director meeting with us to clarify their needs.

Diagnosis. The initial meeting with the director took place one week prior to the group consultation. At this meeting, the three of us discussed the history of the concerns and details about the need for funding for interns. The director also shared his frustrations about his past attempts and his interest now in seeking outside guidance to help find a workable approach.

In this initial meeting, the director reminded us about the dynamics of the staff, pointing out that the group was very energetic, intelligent and interactive with one another. This was important information for us to keep in mind as we planned our approach. Next, we discussed various approaches and agreed that a more informal, discussion-based approach was most suitable for this group. This approach included a discussion of the politics of funding, our experiences in attempting to get additional funding, and facilitation of the group's generation of ideas using the nominal group technique. Finally, we agreed to plan about an hour and a half at the end of the day to discuss the consultation process in general and have a question and answer time. To further support the staff's goal of learning more about consultation, we videotaped the initial meeting with the director for use at the group consultation meeting. We included teaching points about the consultation process in the videotape to highlight the various aspects which this meeting demonstrated.

Implementation. The group consultation took place at the counseling center and all staff members, including the director, counselors and interns, were present. We opened the meeting by sharing the agenda that we developed in the meeting with the director and confirmed with the group that this indeed was the direction in which they wanted to proceed. Next, we showed selected parts of the videotape of the introductory sessions with the director so the group would have the same background on the case. The videotape also served to begin the education process on consultation which would be completed during the last hour and a half of the day. A brief discussion processing the video followed.

We then facilitated the group in brainstorming what they wanted and did not want from the consultation. Though several "wants" were identified, the primary one was to have a plan of action by the end of the session. In terms of what they didn't want, they were strong in not wanting to hear remarks such as "it can't be done" and "the bureaucracy is too complicated." They wanted to be "possibility thinkers" and did not want us to stifle that process! We expressed to them our understanding of what they were saying and agreed to facilitate them in that vein.

Next, we solicited their input and discussion of what their goals were related to the consultation. The group as a whole was very clear that their goal was to increase the staffing of the center so that they could offer additional programs. This was a somewhat broader goal than was originally stated, but was a positive revelation in that it permitted broader options when we brainstormed possible approaches. Even though this goal allowed for options other than funded interns, that was still the primary driver and, as we processed options, was seen as one of the most viable. Further, this goal recognized:

1. the staff's interest in increasing the services offered by the center;
2. the center's role on campus as a training ground for psychology and counseling graduate students; and
3. the staff's strong desire to attract quality students to intern positions at the center.

At this point, we discussed the background of their work to date in searching for funding. This included the director distributing a timeline narrative of his discussions and results with various administrators over the past several years. This was helpful since not all of the staff members, especially interns, were familiar with the detailed history of this issue. We sensed, through the discussion that followed the director's review of the past work, that there was a feeling of frustration and a sense of not knowing what to do next, which was what had drawn them to seek consultation from us.

Although we had planned to use the nominal group technique to provide a structured framework for brainstorming, the dynamics of

105

the group led easily to an informal brainstorming session which proved very fruitful. The sophistication and knowledge base of the group made the use of a more highly structured process such as nominal group technique unnecessary. So we adjusted our plan.

The brainstorming generated a long list of possible routes to achieve additional staff and funding for interns. Next, we grouped the items according to the campus administrative area that would be involved (e.g. academic affairs, student affairs, development, etc.). Our next step was to turn this list into an action plan. We accomplished this by reviewing the list one item at a time and soliciting the group for consensus on who, what, and when for each.

The group recognized that implementation of this plan was an ongoing process and that results would probably be slow in coming. This was recognized especially in light of the university operating on an academic school year basis for budgeting. That is, even if funding was found, it would probably not get into the budget until the following school year. Nevertheless, the group seemed energized to pursue their action plan and we expressed a willingness to come back at some future date to explore their progress.

Having heard from the group that they felt this topic was adequately covered, we became teachers again, reviewing the consultation process and soliciting questions. We used specific elements of the consultation with the group to illustrate the consultation process and techniques.

Disengagement. Since we were not going to actually see the group through the entire implementation process, we processed the consultation at the end of the group session. To get the discussion started, we solicited feedback from the group on the consultation and our performance as consultants.

The group was pleased and felt that they had met the goals of the consultation; they had an action plan for acquiring additional staff/funding and they had been educated on the consultation process.

One staff member did express confusion over our initial plan to use nominal group technique and the fact that we did not use it or the flip chart instruction sheet for that technique that had been posted on the wall prior to the start of the session. We expressed our understanding of her concern and explained that the group had moved so smoothly into brainstorming and was proceeding with it so well, that we thought the more structured approach was not necessary. We also recognized to the group that it might have been less confusing if we had explained this at the time we made the adjustment. The group agreed that that approach would have been helpful.

Implications for Practice

This process consultation leads to several general messages regarding consultation with groups and organizations. When working with a group, you are not one of them, but in some ways you are. There is a strong urge to pick a side and become a player, but it is important for the consultant to resist the temptation to jump into the dynamics and politics of a situation and instead to remain objective. On the other hand, the group needs to see you on some level as part of the team, as a collaborator, as someone who truly understands their issue. In this way, the consultant needs to relate to the group and find some common ground of interest or experience which can unite the consultant and the group. This situation was somewhat eased for us in this consultation because we were already acquainted with the staff and had developed a positive working relationship. We did have to put energy into maintaining a balanced, objective stance as we processed options, particularly in light of the staff's wish that we not stifle their process with "it can't be done" type remarks.

Another message that we can learn about consultation from this case is the use of strong process skills and flexibility. As with so many organizational consultations, at the counseling center there were many players with many ideas. Our use of strong process skills kept the group on track and yet permitted exploration, allowing everyone to contribute and be heard. This was especially true in light of the fact that there were four levels of employees in the group: manager (the center's director), supervisor (one of the counselors who acts as a lead person), direct workers (counselors), and apprentices (interns). For example, during the brainstorming, we noticed that one of the interns was being very quiet and not active in generating ideas. When this was observed, we made a special effort to draw her into the process and solicit her input. Consequently, the intern began sharing and generated a couple of very creative ideas which were added to the action plan.

In terms of flexibility, we changed our plan during the consultation in response to our observations about the group. Had we not been flexible in letting go of the original plan to use nominal group technique, the group might have felt stifled. This could have resulted in resistance to further techniques and discussion through such behaviors as shutting down (passive resistance) or disagreeing with our facilitation (active resistance). As indicated in the disengagement discussion, we did not communicate to the group that we were changing direction and this caused some confusion. In the future, when we have shared an agenda with a group and then decide to change it, we will share this with the group at the time and solicit their support.

In this particular consultation, knowledge of the system in which the organization was operating was very helpful. It permitted us to assist in assessing options and prompting the generation of options. It also provided us the basis to share our own experiences and do

108

so in a manner in which the group could relate. Whether a consultant is part of the system in which he/she consults or not, it is important that the consultant have some background and understanding of the dynamics of the larger organization. Further, the consultant needs to be aware of the norms and vocabulary of the organization and use that in communicating with the consultees. Clearly, consultants should avoid using their own jargon as it may distance them from the consultees or cause confusion.

Consultants need to be open to feedback during and after the consultation. It is easy to hear the positive feedback, but not so easy to hear the things one could have done better. But this is how we improve as consultants and how the consultees become our teachers. Being receptive and non-defensive is especially important in groups because the group may sometimes appear to "gang up" on the consultant, uniting around a point of feedback. In this case, we solicited feedback from the group and made a point to be open and receptive to it. This was particularly important when the staff member shared with us that she was confused with the fact that we did not use nominal group technique. Instead of becoming defensive, we heard her message, agreed with her, and suggested that it might have been helpful if we had let the group know we were changing plans and why. She agreed, felt heard, and we learned a valuable lesson.

In addition to soliciting feedback, consultants can themselves point out areas in which they feel the consultation could have been improved. We did this by expressing that we probably should have given the director more time to discuss and explain the timeline narrative which he distributed. Had we done this, everyone would have had a clearer idea of the types of things that had been tried. As it was, we ended up spending some time during brainstorming removing ideas which had been generated but which had already been tried. This approach of discussing our own areas for improvement showed our genuineness as consultants and the

109

true investment we had in facilitating the most useful outcomes. The consultees commented on our sharing as enhancing our trustworthiness in their eyes even more.

A final area for thought is that of which parties-at-interest to include in preliminary sessions. In this case, at the request of the counseling center staff, we conducted the preliminary exploration with the director only. Though the staff was comfortable with the director representing them, it might have been more helpful if all parties had been present initially. In that case, we all would have had a solid understanding of the background and issues in the case from all perspectives. As it was, we processed these with the director in the initial meeting and then with the staff at the group consultation. Therefore the staff did not have the opportunity to hear the details of the director's perspectives and we did not have time to recreate these or play the entire videotape in the group consultation. Though this point did not pose a large problem with this particular consultation, it could pose a very large problem in organizations where hidden agendas and power games are prevalent. This was not the case at the counseling center.

References and Suggested Readings

Dougherty. A. M., (1995). Consultation; Practice and Perspectives in School and Community Settings. (2nd ed.). Pacific Grove, CA: Brooks/Cole (Chapters 8 and 9).

Kuh, G. D. (1993). Appraising the character of a college. Journal of Counseling & Development, 71, 661-668.

Randolph, D. L., & Graun, K. (1988). Resistance to consultation: A synthesis for counselor-consultants. Journal of Counseling and Development, 67, 182-184.

Rockwood, G. F. (1993). Edgar Schein's process versus content consultation models. Journal of Counseling and Development, 71, 636-638.

Ross, G. J. (1993). Peter Block's flawless consulting and the homunculus theory: Within each person is a perfect consultant. Journal of Counseling and Development, 71, 639-641.

Schein, E. H. (1978). The role of the consultant: Content expert or process facilitator? Personnel and Guidance Journal, 56 (6), 339-343.

Schein, E. H. (1987). Process consultation: Lessons for managers and consultants. Volume II. Reading, MA: Addison-Wesley.

Schein, E. H. (1988). Process consultation: Its role in organization development. Volume I. Reading, MA: Addison-Wesley.

Westbrook, F. D., Kandell, J. J., Kirkland, S. E., Phillips, P. E., Regan, A. M., Medvene, A., & Oslin, Y. D. (1993). University campus consultation: Opportunities and limitations. Journal of Counseling and Development, 76, 684-688.

Editor's Note: Now that you have read this case, reflect upon it and develop a list of five things you might have done differently if you were a consultant involved with the case.

CHAPTER SEVEN

PROCESS CONSULTATION IN A

HEALTH CARE SETTING

Elizabeth Becker-Reems

Setting and Background Issues

Setting. This case study is a composite of several consultation experiences that I had while working in a 400-bed acute care community hospital located in the southeastern United States. The successful and progressive hospital possesses values and a culture that include respect for the individual and investment in people. I had worked in the hospital for several years in personnel and human resource development (HRD) before I started to function in the role of internal consultant. As part of my graduate program in Human Resource Development, I had taken a course in consultation.

Background. In our organization, process consultation services were relatively new. Very few people knew that the Human Resource Division provided internal consulting because we weren't really marketing this service. Since consultation is typically private in nature, the successes we had were known only at the senior management level. Most of our consultation assignments came from the top levels in the organization, a questionable procedure at best.

I had learned through the hospital grapevine that there were personnel problems in the Respiratory Therapy Department. Turnover was high and our job posting system frequently had management and staff vacancies posted for Respiratory Therapy. Consequently, I wasn't surprised when I received a call asking me to attend a meeting with the vice president in charge of Respiratory Therapy as well as the director of the Respiratory Therapy Department to discuss a possible consultation.

Consultation Goals

The primary goal of this consultation was to help the consultee gain insight into the everyday events in the organization and act on those events constructively. As you will note later on in this case, the specific goals the consultee set had significant implications for the consultee changing his own behavior. The primary goal was to enhance the overall effectiveness of the Respiratory Therapy Department and consequently that of the entire hospital.

Consultant Function and Roles

As a process consultant, my major roles in this consultation were those of facilitator and catalyst. I also functioned as a collaborator with the consultee such that our consultation became a joint effort. As a process consultant, I provided less structure and direct input than would a consultant operating from a more expert mode. I tended to focus not only on what was being done, but also on how those things were being done (Schein, 1987, 1988).

Consultee's Experience in Consultation

The consultee functioned as an active collaborator in this consultation. Although the consultee himself became the primary target of change, he defined the diagnostic steps that led to goal setting and action plans. He functioned as an active problem solver during the entire consultation process. It was assumed that the entire organization would benefit from the changes the consultee made (Dougherty, 1995). Hopefully, the changes the consultee made would reduce the necessity of my being involved with him in a similar situation in the future.

Application: Consultation Techniques and Procedures

<u>Entry</u>. <u>A Meeting to Explore Possibilities</u>. I took my pen and note pad and went to the meeting. It was held in the vice president's office and would likely last about an hour. It would not be a meeting of strangers. I had worked with the vice president on several similar projects. I had come to know the director of Respiratory Therapy in the three years he had worked at the hospital. He and I had worked on a special assignment during his first year, served on some of the same task forces, and attended management-level social functions together. I was wondering how serious the problem was, and how he would view consultation.

After several minutes of congenial social talk, the vice president stated the purpose of the meeting. "Liz, I have asked you here to meet with Larry and me to talk about helping him improve the situation in the Respiratory Therapy Department. Larry and I have some ideas of what might be going wrong, but we would like some outside help. I've talked to your boss, and he is willing for you to work with us, if you have the time. I believe you can be of assistance."

I asked the vice president to explain the problem in more detail. Apparently, two long-term supervisors in the department had tried to "back-door" the director (Larry) and go without his consent directly to the vice president for help in improving the work environment in the Respiratory Therapy Department. The vice president was already familiar with the problems in the department. In weekly meetings with the director, the vice president had learned about the department's high rate of turnover, the frustrations the director was experiencing in trying to make improvements in the department, and the department's severe morale problem.

Regarding the high rate of turnover, qualified respiratory therapists were hard to find and salaries were very competitive. It was not unusual for registered therapists to work at a hospital for two years, and them move on to a more desirable location with higher pay. Because of the state of the economy and the scarcity of qualified registered therapists, they could more or less choose where they worked. The director and the vice president had the therapists' pay level reviewed by the personnel office on a regular basis and had determined that competitive pay was not a factor with turnover. The director then expressed the concern that he couldn't determine a solution to the current level of turnover. He did think, however, that part of the problem might be the level of dissatisfaction among several "old-timers" who had been employed at the hospital for many years. The director was concerned about the incident of "back-dooring" by the supervisors. He noted that there was a history of his supervisors not conferring with him about the department's problems. We then discussed other problems the department was experiencing such as the state of its morale.

At this point, I suggested that consultation may be of some benefit in ameliorating one or more of the problems we had been discussing. We reviewed the highlights of the consultation process and discussed how the consultation between Larry and me might proceed. As we talked I outlined the basic steps on my note pad. I later gave Larry a copy of the steps. I then spent some time discussing confidentiality. I did this deliberately to make sure the vice president would not pressure me to share information about the consultation and to fulfill my ethical objective to acquire Larry's informed consent.

Larry had not worked with an internal consultant before yet didn't ask any questions during the meeting. His lack of responsiveness made me feel uncomfortable and caused me to wonder whether Larry really wanted to be involved in a consultation relationship with me. So I asked, "Larry, do you think there will be any benefit to us working together?" He spoke up and asserted that he really did need some help and wanted to engage in consultation. Although I still sensed some hesitation from him, I decided not to pursue it at this time. I kept sensing that he was feeling pressure from the vice president to engage in consultation.

I felt that it was important to clarify with whom I would be working during consultation. I was concerned about how the vice president was going to fit into all of this. If the vice president was bent on "micromanaging" my consultation, the fact that he was Larry's immediate supervisor could have disastrous results on the consultation. So I asked the vice president, "After our meeting today, I will be working directly with Larry. Is that correct? And how will you be involved?" The vice president stated that it was an assignment for Larry and me, and that he would rely on Larry to give him progress updates. I made a note of that. From past experience, I knew that communicating with the vice president would be an important part of Larry's role but something that I would rather avoid. The meeting adjourned with the agreement that additional data gathering on the problems was needed. Larry and I decided to meet again the next day to further discuss consultation and develop a plan for our work together.

<u>Follow-up to the Exploratory Meeting</u>. When I got back to my office after the meeting, I created a file for the Respiratory Therapy Department consultation. The file included notes from my meeting with the vice president and Larry along with some observations I had made about Larry. As I prepared the file, I realized that I did not know whether the vice president had any expectations about the length of the consultation and what specific results he expected. These insights made me wonder if I was being too dependent on trying to read the vice president's mind on these issues rather than involving Larry in making decisions about them.

I asked the personnel office to provide me with a list of all the employees in the Respiratory Therapy Department along with their job titles and employment dates. I added this information to my file which helped give me a sense of the make-up of the department. I decided not to gather any other data until Larry and I had our first meeting and decided what information was necessary.

I believed that my first meeting alone with Larry would be critical to how well we would relate during my consultation. I wanted to help Larry feel comfortable with me and the consultation process. Based on my observations at the meeting with the vice president, I felt Larry wasn't sure about the process. I also believed that he did not have confidence in my abilities to assist him. I felt the need to build up my credibility in Larry's eyes. I drew up a brief agenda for the first meeting I would have with Larry. I would go over the agenda with Larry at the beginning of our meeting and seek his approval to follow it. The agenda looked like this:

1. Share some of my educational and consultation experiences with Larry to build up my credibility in his eyes.
2. Ask Larry to redefine the problem from his perspective.

3.   Ask Larry what his expectations were for the length of the consultation relationship.
4.   Come to an agreement concerning what roles each of us would take on during consultation.
5.   Determine what Larry expected to get out of consultation.
6.   Develop a preliminary plan for ameliorating the identified problems.
7.   Ask Larry what he believed his vice president's expectations were for both results and length of the consultation and if these expectations placed any barriers on our work together.
8.   Ask Larry how he planned to keep his vice president informed of any progress.

As I reviewed the proposed agenda, I anticipated that the meeting would take approximately two hours.

Our First Session. My office, along with all the other personnel and human resource development facilities, was located in a building separate from the main hospital. Larry and I agreed to meet in my office. As I had anticipated, Larry was hesitant about having me meet with him in his office. As Larry talked, I sensed that he felt inadequate as a manager because he could not solve the problems facing his department by himself. So I initiated discussion of how major organizations such as AT&T and Xerox have their top levels of management rely on the services of internal and external consultants to deal with problems and growth issues.

I tried to clarify for Larry how he might benefit from consultation. I wanted him to know that experiencing consultation was a learning process, and after being a consultee this one time, he would acquire the foundation of a system that he could use for future problem solving. I wanted him to know that we would be collaborating partners, working together on solving the department's problems, and that all important decisions would be his. I also indicated that my involvement might well save him time, provide him with a sounding board, and allow him to gather more information than he might be able to obtain alone. Finally, we discussed the idea that either of us could terminate the consulting relationship without any "fallout."

We then came up with a reasonably clear statement of the problems to be dealt with during consultation. These problems included:

* The turnover rate in the Respiratory Therapy Department was higher than desirable.
* Departmental morale appeared to be at an all time low.
* "Back-dooring" was being engaged in by some of the supervisors as well as Larry himself.
* The night shift was unhappy and felt ignored.
* Two long-term supervisors were perceived by Larry as having a generally negative attitude toward the department.

These problems turned out to be multi-faceted. We didn't know if these were symptoms of a larger problem or problems in their own right. We wouldn't know the extent of the problem until we completed gathering data.

In planning our work together, I walked Larry through the steps of the consultation process. I provided him with copies of some of Edgar Schein's (1987, 1988) works. We determined that this project might take four to six months if we devoted several hours to it each week. We did not set a firm termination date as we felt that we needed more information to determine the scope of problems to be attacked.

<u>Diagnosis.</u> We decided to gather some preliminary data. I would get data about the departmental employees from the personnel

119

department. Larry would put some subjective data together based on his knowledge of the department, its people and its problems. In addition, Larry was to generate a list of employees and identify those whom he believed were positive about the department and the work environment, those who were unclear, and those who were slightly or very negative. It was during this stage that I finally got the feeling that Larry and I were "clicking" as a team. It was almost as if my nonjudgmental attitude rippled over to Larry and allowed him to be less judgmental about himself, others in the department and me.

For my part, I obtained turnover data for the last five years from the Personnel Office by job type in the department, by shift, and for the department as a whole. In addition, I retrieved copies of exit interviews for the past year. Once I had gathered my data, I analyzed it to see if there were any trends or items of interest. I noted that there was no turnover in the clerical staff for the last five years and little among the technicians. Where turnover was unusually high was among the registered respiratory therapists who had been hired in the last three years, the supervisors, and the people who worked the night shift. This exit interview data identified the following as the contributing reasons for leaving the organization: lack of trust, lack of commitment of the director to his staff, and the undesirability of working the night shift.

Our Second Session. Larry and I met again to review the data we had gathered. Larry's review of his subjective data indicated problems with five out of seven supervisors; four out of five night shift employees, and more than half of the registered respiratory therapists. As we discussed the implications of the data, Larry indicated that he felt the basic issue was that the supervisors were working against him. If he could only get rid of several long-term supervisors whom Larry believed were undermining him, then the work environment of the department would improve. The more Larry and I talked, the more I realized that he was accepting little or no responsibility for contributing to the problems in the

120

department. He did recognize, however, that getting rid of several long-term supervisors was not a viable solution. I then shared the data I had gathered from the personnel office. I suggested that Larry and I focus primarily on the exit interview information. The issues of lack of trust and commitment of the director to the staff seemed to hit Larry like a sledge hammer. He suggested the possibility of gathering more data from the current members of the department because he was certain that it was "just those two supervisors who were stirring up all the trouble." So we agreed to gather one more set of data by interviewing all the supervisors, several registered therapists, and all the night shift workers.

Together we designed the interview questions for the current employees. At Larry's request, I agreed to conduct the interviews. We agreed that the results of the interviews would be shared with Larry, all of the supervisors, the night shift employees and those respiratory therapists who were interviewed.

The Interviews. Larry introduced me to the employees in the department at a regularly scheduled staff meeting. Larry said that I was there to help improve the work environment through data gathering, analysis and problem solving. He expressed his commitment to improving the environment in the department and reducing turnover. There was no discussion by the employees. I could sense the level of distrust within the department. I scheduled meetings with each of the supervisors and began interviewing them. I planned an hour for each interview. After interviewing the supervisors, I interviewed the registered therapists, and then the night shift employees.

As it turned out, Larry was mistrusted by all but two supervisors. However, even those two supervisors accurately corroborated the problems that the other supervisors described. Apparently, Larry himself was guilty of "back-dooring" in his relationships with his supervisors. If Larry wanted to involve an employee in a project, he would go directly to the employee. The supervisor might not learn of the employee's involvement until the project was underway. If the supervisor attempted discipline and the disciplined employee came to Larry, he might reinterpret the problem and dismiss the disciplinary action that was taken by the supervisor. Consequently, the supervisors saw no problem with their own "back-dooring" behavior.

In addition, Larry was viewed as spending very little time in the department. Many employees alleged that he spent most of his time enhancing his relationship with his peers such as the doctors and nurses at the hospital, building a state-wide reputation for himself, and making himself look good to senior management. The basic message seemed to be: "A good department head stays home and Larry doesn't 'stay home!'" Several of the people I interviewed noted that Larry had a bad habit of using the word "I" frequently in his conversations with others. This gave the impression that he cared more about himself than the problems and people in the department. The supervisors and all of the others I interviewed agreed that Larry was very intelligent, charming and forward-thinking. However they did not trust him and they did not like working with him. They also claimed that he was cold, insensitive, and manipulative in his communications. The supervisors were even losing respect for senior management because the communication problems had been there for a long time with senior management having done nothing to alleviate them.

Based on the interviews, it appeared that the supervisors were willing to work on the problems as a group as long as they had some assurance that Larry would also be willing to change his behavior. The issues with the night shift employees seemed tangential to the emerging problem. The night shift reported little contact with Larry. They were primarily unhappy with working the night shift and felt there was little attention or recognition from Larry. Based on all of this additional information from these interviews, I determined that Larry was going to have to face a reality different from the one that he perceived. I planned my next meeting with Larry carefully. I could see Larry rejecting the information, rejecting me as a supporter, and rejecting the entire consultation process. In my interviews, I had obtained specific examples of the problems as seen by the supervisors and other employees. I hoped the specifics would help Larry understand the problems and prevent him from dismissing them as glib generalities.

Our Third Session. When Larry and I met, we reviewed the information from the interviews, along with the data from the personnel office, and Larry's assessment of the morale of the people in his department. I already had drawn some conclusions from the data but wanted to see what Larry thought about this new information.

As it turned out, Larry was dismayed by the results of the interviews. After reviewing the information, he sat silently for a few moments. I then suggested that we look at each item and test the validity of the supervisors' perceptions. He bought the idea. We started talking about what he had been able to accomplish while spending time with the nurses and doctors at the hospital. He stated that he didn't see his role as spending all his time in the department and that progress would stop if he wasn't out negotiating with managers and physicians in the organization every day. We talked about the reputation of the department in the state and the region. He said that the department was highly regarded as professional and forward-thinking, providing challenging work and an opportunity to collaborate with physicians and other health care providers.

Then we got to the "bad news." I asked about his role within the department and his support of the supervisors. He said that he hadn't realized that he had been "back-dooring" the supervisors, but as he listened to the examples they shared, he knew that what the supervisors were saying was accurate. He asked me if I noticed that he "over-used" the word "I" so much in his conversation. I had to reply that I had noticed that he used the word frequently. He said he was concerned about that and that he might try to count the number of times he used "I" in a brief conversation and consider using "we" more. At that point Larry more or less "caved in" and said, "Maybe I am the one who has to change first if we are going to get anywhere."

Based on this discussion we then agreed on and set the following goals:

1. Clarify the organizational structure of the department by assessing the roles and responsibilities of the personnel in the department (with a particular emphasis on the roles of Larry and the supervisors).
2. Spread ownership for the effectiveness of the department to the supervisors by involving them in choosing departmental priorities and strategies for improvement.
3. Improve Larry's own interpersonal communication skills so that he would be perceived as a more sensitive and less self-centered administrator by the department's employees.
4. Improve the professional relationships that Larry had with the supervisors.
5. Discontinue any "back-dooring" by departmental employees.

We evaluated the goals and determined that they were very ambitious. Larry and I knew we needed supervisor involvement and agreed to finalize the goals after a subsequent meeting with the supervisors. We also took this opportunity to discuss the nature of feedback as an intervention in itself, and how the feedback session could start to bridge the communication gap among Larry and the supervisors.

The Feedback Session. Larry decided to lead the session even though it was somewhat threatening to him to do so. We shared the information that he and I had gathered. It turned out to be a very uncomfortable meeting for everyone involved, but at the same time there was a sense of hope and an atmosphere of honesty that had been missing in recent departmental interactions. As it turned out, many of the employees seemed pleasantly surprised that Larry owned some of the responsibility for the problems the department was experiencing. Several employees spoke up concerning the various goals that should be pursued to enhance the department's effectiveness. There appeared to be unanimous support for clarifying the department's organizational structure in terms of roles and resonsibilities. Several employees voiced an opinion that the whole communication system in the department "stank." Several people suggested that the communication system be changed. No one implied that Larry should be replaced.

Our Fourth Session. After the meeting, Larry and I spent two hours in my office unwinding and rehashing the meeting. It had been a long and difficult day. Larry and I had achieved a new level of trust and understanding. It was as if he understood that people didn't want a different director, just a changed Larry. They would be willing to change if he would. With one addition, the goals that we came away with after the meeting were much the same as we had previously agreed upon. The supervisors believed that the communication system in the department was ineffective. It was decided that a focus group made up of some members of the department would be formed and charged to assess the communication system and recommend improvements.

Implementation. Our Fifth Session. Larry and I met the following week. We took the goals we had previously set and brainstormed

125

interventions. After extensive discussion, we selected the interventions listed below:

GOAL #1: Clarify the organizational structure of the department by assessing the roles and responsibilities of the personnel in the department (with a particular emphasis on those of Larry and the supervisors).

INTERVENTION: Role Clarification

    a.   Clarify the role of director, supervisors, registered respiratory therapists, office support, and respiratory technicians.
    b.   Facilitate the role clarification process.
    c.   Develop revised job descriptions.
    d.   Communicate revised job descriptions to appropriate parties-at-interest.

INTERVENTION: Restructure the Department Communication Process

    a.   Select a task force of departmental employees.
    b.   Determine the types of meetings needed, chairperson, attendees, minutes, frequency and agenda possibilities.
    c.   Determine what goes in mail boxes, what goes on bulletin boards, and who is responsible for maintaining these systems.
    d.   Revise and implement an improved orientation program for new employees.

GOAL #2: Spread ownership for the effectiveness of the department to the supervisors by involving them in choosing departmental priorities and strategies for improvement.

126

INTERVENTION: Conduct a Feedback Session with Supervisors

    a.   Feedback data gathered and interview results to supervisors.

    b.   Have supervisors provide feedback or selected consultation goals and revise goals as necessary.

GOAL #3:   Improve Larry's interpersonal communication skills so that he would be perceived as a more sensitive and less self-centered administrator.

INTERVENTION: Communication and Sensitivity Training for the Director

    a.   Identify alternative training opportunities.

    b.   Select an opportunity.

    c.   Schedule and attend the training.

    d.   Modify behavior.

    e.   Give feedback on the behavior.

GOAL #4:   Improve the professional relationships that Larry has with the supervisors.

INTERVENTION: Team Building among the Management Team

    a.   Decide on the team-building activities.

    b.   Schedule and communicate the team-building sessions.

    c.   Conduct the activities.

GOAL #5:   Discontinue any "back-dooring" by anyone in the department.

INTERVENTION: Personal Commitment

We developed a time frame for these interventions. We included regular "How's it going?" meetings between Larry and me. In addition, we included periodic updates to Larry's vice president. These updates were Larry's responsibility and I got little feedback about them during the course of our consultation relationship.

Disengagement. Subsequent Sessions. At our "How's it going?" meetings we adjusted the time line and talked about the reception the various interventions were receiving in his department. By now, Larry had the supervisors involved in conducting some of the sessions and I was becoming less involved in the implementation.

As part of the evaluation process, I was interested in identifying my own strengths and shortcomings in the consultation process. So I had asked for feedback from Larry as we progressed. Was I clear in communicating with him? Was I responding to him and his department in a timely manner? Was I sensitive to his needs and concerns? Did he believe the exercises we did were helpful, harmful, or just time-consuming? Was I staying within my role as collaborator, or did I step out of it and give advice? As the consultation drew to a close, I wanted to know what Larry's overall perceptions were. We agreed to meet and give each other some feedback.

Larry was glad to see the consultation come to an end. He said that he felt like his behavior was under a microscope and that he felt tremendous pressure. He said that the best thing I did as a consultant was when he asked for advice to suggest that we brainstorm together, rather than give him easy solutions. He liked the give and take of collaboration, and noted that he would miss that. He said that being able to come to my office whenever he wanted and just talk about what was happening helped a lot. We agreed to update each other every two weeks for the next two months to see how things were progressing. He asked me to let him know if I heard him use the word "I" frequently in his conversation. It had become something of a joke to us.

I had also established a relatively close relationship with several of the supervisors. I told them I would come to a few of their management team meetings in order to keep posted on how things were going. I knew I would miss my meetings and appointments with Respiratory Therapy. But that's a part of what consultation is all about.

Near the end of the formal consultation relationship, Larry and I wrote a brief report of our consultation experience. He gave a copy to his vice president and I gave one to mine.

Implications For Practice

The consultation experience outlined in this chapter has a number of implications for practice. First and foremost, each time I conduct a consultation, I typically learn something new that I can apply when I am involved in a subsequent consultation relationship. For example, from this consultation I realized that working with a person as the "primary" consultee does not negate involvement with other consultees. This consultation was with the department director and was designed to help him solve problems with his supervisors and staff. However, as the consultation progressed, the supervisors became direct as well as indirect recipients of consultative services. Since the consultation lasted almost six months, relationships were formed with the supervisors as well as with the director. Those relationships enhanced the quality of the consultation experience for me, provided learning opportunities for the supervisors, and assured a more lasting impact from the consultation.

Second, consultants need to be proactive in marketing their services. This is important in order for internal consultants to receive recognition and to achieve credibility within the organization. Most middle and senior managers in health care have little or no experience with process consultation. The very thought of looking at how things are done can be threatening because it places the focus on people's behavior rather than concepts like "bureaucratic structures." In order to use process consultation effectively, managers need to learn what it is, the benefits it provides, and the qualifications necessary for internal consultants to effectively conduct it. In addition, when internal consultants effectively market their services, the entry stage will be easier and the number of requests for consultation will most likely increase.

Consultants need to be careful not to expand the scope of the consultation project beyond what the consultee wants to achieve. However, in certain process consultations, neither the consultee nor the consultant can clearly define the scope of the project without first gathering data. Initially, it appeared as though two long-term supervisors with negative attitudes were disrupting the department and creating an unacceptable work environment. Through the interview process and the involvement of the supervisors, it became clear that there were a variety of "causes" of the problems, and that one of those causes was the consultee himself.

It is critical to take the time to gather the type of information needed to increase the likelihood for a successful outcome to consultation. The need to look at the organizational structure and roles of the supervisors in the department was most apparent from the data from exit interviews. Larry's involvement in the department's problems only became apparent after interviewing the supervisors and several employees. Individual interviews are a very rich source of data and, though time-consuming, frequently provide pertinent information that cannot be gathered elsewhere.

Consultants need to stress the benefits and learning opportunities from participating in consultation at its outset. In order to maintain the self-esteem of the consultee and to assure the success of any remedies or solutions that are eventually implemented, consultees themselves need to be in charge of the change process from the outset of the consultation relationship. Collaboration is an essential tool to accomplish this. In this case, Larry did not see himself in charge of the consultation process at the beginning. When his vice president suggested he use my consultation services, Larry perceived the suggestion as an order, not merely an idea. Larry needed to be able to see the benefits to himself in order to take ownership of the process. If he had not accepted the consultation process, it would not have been effective.

Formative evaluation is very important in process consultation. At the beginning of the consultation, I told Larry that one of the benefits of the process would be learning. During the consultation relationship we need to remember to take the time to process with consultees what has transpired. This process facilitates the enhancement of the problem-solving skills of the consultee.

Consultation needs to be viewed as a desirable and legitimate enterprise within the organization. Larry initially resisted the idea of involving an internal consultant to help solve the problems in his department. He saw needing help as a personal weakness and did not recognize that using internal resources effectively could be a productive management technique. It appears that consultation is frequently used in organizations "when all else fails," and when the potential consultee is getting desperate. Consultation should be used like other problem solving strategies - as a part of our daily work life. Then it would become a more acceptable endeavor in which managers and other prospective consultees might engage.

References and Suggested Readings

Cooper, S. E., and O'Connor, Jr., R. M. (1993). Standards for organizational consultation assessment and evaluation investments. Journal of Counseling and Development, 71, 651-660.

Dougherty, A.M. (1995). Consultation: Practice and perspectives in school and community settings. (2nd Ed.). Pacific Grove, CA: Brooks/Cole. (Chapters 8 and 9).

Fyqua, D. R., and Kurpius, D. J. (1993). Conceptual models in organizational consultation. Journal of Counseling and Development, 71, 607-618.

Hansen, J. C., Himes, B.S., and Meier, S. (1990). Consultation: Concepts and practices. Englewood Cliffs, NJ: Prentice Hall. (Chapter 5).

Rockwood, G. F. (1993). Edgar Schein's process versus content consultation models. Journal of Counseling and Development, 71, 636-638.

Schein, E. H. (1987). Process consultation: Lessons for managers and consultants. Volume II. Reading, MA: Addison-Wesley.

Schein, E.H. (1988). Process consultation: Its role in organization development. Volume I. Reading, MA: Addison-Wesley.

Schein, E.H. (1990). Organizational culture. American Psychologist, 45, 109-119.

Editor's Note: Now that you have read this case, reflect upon it and develop a list of five things you might have done differently if you were a consultant involved with the case.

CHAPTER EIGHT

SYSTEMS CONSULTATION: WORKING WITH

A METROPOLITAN POLICE DEPARTMENT

Dick James, Walter Crews and Burl Gilliland

Setting and Background Issues

Setting. Shelby City has a large, complex police department that has all of the tasks and crimes that face a contemporary metropolitan city of over a million people. It also has a large population of mentally ill individuals who are in the custodial care of relatives and intermediate care facilities. Additionally there are scores of mentally ill homeless, psychotic substance abusers, recently released parolees with mental distubances, mental hospital patients, and other people with a variety of physical and emotional problems that often lead to irrational behaviors that are acted out in the homes and streets of Shelby City.

Since Shelby City police officers do not consider the mentally ill to be "crooks," many feel that the requirement to respond to "mental case" calls is not a true law enforcement responsibility. As a result, the message that "This is not my job! " crosses their minds and they want to get these calls over with as quickly as possible by whatever means necessary. Therefore, to propose a program that would change their views and operating procedures toward controlling the acting out mentally ill was met initially with a good deal of caution, pessimism, and cynicism by the rank and file of the Shelby City Police Department. It was into this emotionally charged setting of intense political pressure and forced compliance to change that the consultants were called. Thus, this case study describes the systems consultation framework that resulted in the development of a program of police patrol officers being selected, trained, and deployed as crisis interventionists for the specific purpose of safely and effectively controlling the severe expressive behaviors of the violent mentally ill.

Background. To get a sense of the background issues related to this case consider the following scenario: A deranged man is standing in the middle of a public housing development in Shelby City, stabbing himself repeatedly with a butcher knife, screaming incoherently, and making threatening gestures to neighbors. The police arrive on the scene and attempt to bring the situation under control and take the man into custody. Over the next thirty minutes, more and more police arrive on the scene. Finally, the man lunges at police officers with the butcher knife, is shot repeatedly, and dies enroute to the hospital. A huge public outcry ensues, advocacy groups demonstrate against police brutality, the media launches attacks on the police department, lawsuits are filed against the city, and the police department experiences political pressure from the city administration to do something about their apparent ineptness in handling the mentally ill.

Police officers are generally trained to deal with instrumental crimes which involve the gain of some material end by a criminal. Catching bank robbers, car thieves, dope pushers, and other fleeing felons is the stereotypical notion of what policework is. However, about 85% of all police calls in the United States do not involve "catching crooks."

134

The great majority of police calls involve <u>expressive</u> crimes where smoldering emotions often erupt into violence. Domestic problems, sexual assault, barroom brawls, neighborhood quarrels, and the acting out mentally ill all fall into the <u>expressive</u> crime category. Expressive crimes are frustrating, problematic, and very dangerous to police officers because the sole goal of the perpetrator is the attempt to reduce emotional tension by any means possible. As a result, behavior is highly unpredictable and controlling it is complicated by the fact that police officers receive little training in how to deal with expressive crime and safely controlling the violent mentally ill.

Consultation Goals

Our primary goal as consultants was to enhance the functioning of the police department in delivering services to one of its constituencies (in this case the violently mentally ill). To attain this goal, we would be working not only with the police department, but with the total ecological system of mental health provision in Shelby City. Like in any system, each part is interdependent upon the other for effective functioning. Family members, community mental health agency staffs, hospital emergency room personnel, advocacy groups, and professional mental health service providers all play important parts in the safe control of the mentally ill and needed to be brought together with the police department in order for all of them to function more effectively.

To highlight the interactive effects various systems can have on one another, mental health workers, who are the very people the police need most to help tackle how best to deal with the mentally ill, are often viewed by the police as soft-hearted, rose-colored-glasses-view liberals who are entirely out of touch with the reality of the mean streets officers are patrolling. Likewise, mental health professionals are likely to see the police as uncaring, cynical

135

enforcers of brutal and restrictive laws that do little but exacerbate problems for them and their clientele. As a result, each system typically views the other with distrust and suspicion.

Assessment. Assessment of the ecosystem of the mentally ill in Shelby City indicated that there were three clearly defined subsystems interacting within the larger system. First there was a consumer advocacy group, the Alliance for the Mentally Ill. This group is composed mainly of relatives and friends of long-term, chronic psychotics. Besides functioning as a support group for one another, their primary purpose is to lobby for increased social and psychological services for the mentally ill. Their goal is to have police respond quickly to out-of-control relatives, but to do so in a safe and humane manner. At the time of this consultation, the Alliance was extremely irate at the Shelby City police because of a number of mishandled responses to mental disturbance calls.

The second group was comprised of the professional service providers of mental health: the various hospitals, community mental health clinics, and other community service providers that deal on a daily basis with the mentally ill. At the time of this consultation, they believed they did not have a stake in the issue, other than to be wary of their interaction with the police. Their goal is to provide service to the mentally ill as best they can, given the limited resources they have and with as little interference from others as they can get.

The third group was the police department itself. Strategically, its immediate goal is to decrease its negative public image in not being able to deal in a safe, effective manner with the violent mentally ill. Tactically, its goal is to learn new procedures in handling mental disturbance calls so that fast, safe, and effective intervention is possible. Logistically, the department needed to obtain the skills and resources necessary to do so.

136

<u>Initiating Goals</u>. Our first goal was to bring together these often antagonistic and suspicious groups so that a systemic problem-solving process could start to occur. To do that, we attempted to bring all three groups together on a common ground.   This would be a critical first step in convincing them that each had a vested interest in assisting the Shelby City police to deal more effectively with the mentally ill. If we could bring these groups together, then we could use the combined power and creativity of these different subsystems to create a climate for change as well as provide the energy and resources for doing so.

Our second goal was to formulate a training program to teach police officers how to work with the mentally ill so that both parties remained safe and culminated in a positive resolution to the mental disturbance call.

Our third goal had three facets: determine the best way to use the police department in implementing the program; develop strategies to monitor and troubleshoot the program as it went into operation; and determine what additional adjustments, if any, needed to be made.

Our fourth goal was to evaluate the effectiveness of the program by using both quantitative and qualitative outcome measures.

Consultant Role and Function

Consultants who work with systems, particularly systems that may be antagonistic to one another, have several roles. First and foremost, we needed to bring the systems together and establish communication links between them. If this could not be accomplished, then any real or lasting success was unlikely. Second, it was critical that a chairperson for the group be selected who had the trust, respect, and ability to work with and understand the needs, fears, and agendas of each of these groups. The selection of a police command officer who had a graduate degree in human services and was also seen as a credible police officer by the department was an important ingredient in enabling these diverse groups to work with one another. This person was the major communications link between the members of the task group and the police department.

Third, both the administrative hierarchy and rank and file of the targeted systems needed to have enough belief in the need for such a program and its chances of success that they would be willing to submit themselves to change. It is not enough that administrative fiat is used to dictate that rank and file undergo training. When the police are the targeted system for change, veteran officers may be very cynical about what they are being asked to do, particularly when they may be asked to put their lives on the line. Conversely, if the administration is not vitally involved and is merely committing to the program to save face and neutralize political and media pressure, then there is little hope that lasting effects will occur. We needed to convince both commanders and patrol officers that this was a worthwhile endeavor. What we would be calling for was no less than a paradigmatic shift away from a "John Wayne, line up the troops and charge" mentality in dealing with the mentally ill.

We would have to do likewise with the professional staff of the mental health services. There was little money for training. Therefore, training would have to be on a pro bono basis. We would have to convince these professionals that training police officers was worth their time and effort. Besides dealing with some very complex system dynamics, we would be responsible for coordinating assessment efforts to determine what configuration the training and ultimate implementation of the plan would take. We would be in charge of coordinating training. Finally, we were responsible for coordinating follow-up to determine how effective the training was, how effectively the plan was put in operation, and what might need to be done to remediate problem situations as they arose.

Consultee Experience in Consultation

As policing has slowly evolved into a profession in Shelby City and more and more officers have obtained college degrees, there has been a slow raising of consciousness that outside expertise may be a valuable asset - particularly when the issues do not fall within the range of competencies that exist internally within the department. Thus, the police administration was astute enough to understand they had a problem and they needed the support and validation of mental health professionals to deal with it.

Further, since the Shelby City police ran their own police academy, they already had an existing belief in the value of education. They understood that our outside expertise would bring a greater degree of credibility to the program because of our combination of experience in law enforcement, education, and mental health. Our backgrounds made entry into the various systems easier for us than for other consultants who did not have such experiences. We also brought with us an objective, constraint-free perspective which the department would not have, given the considerable political pressure it was under to effect a rapid and effective solution.

In spite of the obvious breach with the traditional role of how police previously dealt with the mentally ill, officers who volunteered for the program reported that they knew the old ways of doing things did not work. While they were unsure if they could master some of the concepts we were proposing and knew that they would have to radically change their thinking about procedures for handling the mentally ill, they were all volunteers who had committed themselves to come into training with an open mind. Therefore, it was important for us to reinforce the police

139

officers for operating in new and divergent ways and, as with learners of any new material, affirm to them that it would be okay to make mistakes, ask questions, and voice concerns over what they were being asked to do. Because the police officers already had experienced going through the police academy, participated in continuing education, and had volunteered to be in the program, they approached training with a healthy skepticism. At the same time, they also brought a good deal of creativity in using the information and training related to calming and defusing techniques. As they carried their learning into the field, they proved to be highly adaptable in turning lectures and modeling of their instructors into practice.

Application: Consultant Techniques and Procedures

Entry. Exploring organizational needs. We wanted to make a comprehensive needs assessment to determine the extent of the problem. To do this, it was necessary for us to bring the different systems together to determine their perceptions of the problem. After determining who would be representative of and could make commitments for the police, the Shelby City Alliance for the Mentally Ill, and a broad array of the Shelby City mental health provider and social service systems, we called a meeting that invited them to become involved in a partnership to help the police deal with the violent mentally ill.

This initial meeting was extremely critical in getting the project on a solid footing. We invited middle- and upper-level managment of the police department, the paramedics, the veterans hospital, the local state mental hospital, emergency rooms, social service agencies, community mental health clinics, the housing authority, the mayor's office, legal representation for the city, and the Alliance for the Mentally Ill to share their concerns with us. The mayor, police chief, and chief executive officer for the city opened the meeting with speeches indicating their support for the project and then gave a charge to the audience to help them. By enlisting the support of these officials, we had hopefully set the stage and impressed the audience with how important this project was to the city. We invited as many human service organizations to this meeting as possible, including those who might only play a tangential role in the development of the program. In an undertaking of this magnitude a number of organizations and individuals may have a great deal of initial zeal, but later fall by the wayside.

We followed up their comments by indicating that this project was so extensive and so critical that no individual organization could handle it alone. Therefore, we needed the cooperation and input from everyone there. We also indicated that there would be no money and probably little recognition for what they were about to commit to do. We deliberately made these statements to head off any turf wars that might have developed in regard to jealousy over what agencies might obtain more money or public recognition.

We were still faced with a selling job. Our continuous focus was on two primary issues: safety for the client as well as the officer and overall improvement of the mental health services delivery system (with special attention given to filling the gap between lethal and nonlethal force). We had to sell the idea that there was something in this for everyone, but to get that "something" everyone needed to hang together. Otherwise, we would all wind up hanging separately! As we expected, a good many suspicious questions and some emotional catharsis arose from the audience. To meet the participants' emotional and security needs, we used an extensive amount of the basic exploration techniques of restatement of content, summary of ideas, open-ended questions, reflection of feelings, and nonjudgmental evaluations of the factual information presented. From our standpoint, this opening meeting involved a great deal of "tuning in" on our parts. Such an effort enabled us to better understand the dynamics of the different groups, their perception of the problem, the part they might play in its solution, and any hidden agendas which might surface.

A good deal of catharsis occurred about the interaction of mental health and the police. We met these complaints in an empathic, affirming way, but constantly repeated the theme that the police-mental health alliance was critical and could not be accomplished without their help. We intentionally used peer pressure and possible loss-of-face in front of one's peers by asking each organization to commit planning and training time to our proposal. We gained their commitment by passing a sheet around for them to write their names on. We then prioritized a list of issues to be discussed and activities to be planned. We divided them into task groups to start working on solutions. We then set a two week turn around time to come back with working drafts of what they were going to do. A strict operational agenda and timeline was adhered to so the planning group would stay highly motivated and on task. We set a tentative future start time of six months to have the program in operation. We pushed hard on both short and long range operational goals and planning times because we wanted participants to know they would have to get busy and stay busy in order to get the program off the ground.

Prior to this meeting we sought to arm ourselves with as many facts as possible so that we might mentally compare what was being said with what we knew to be factual. Therefore, we gained access to the police computer and ascertained the number of mental disturbance calls Shelby City Officers had made in the last year, the number of times additional assistance was needed, how many people were transported to the local mental hospital for emergency commitment, how many reports of client injuries and officer injuries were made, and other statistics that would give us an objective view of the problem. Armed with these facts we were better able to determine the validity of what was being said and make a more accurate analysis of the problem.

142

Contracting. When working across systems, contracting is essential for a variety of reasons. First and foremost, a contract commits the organization and individual to perform particular, specified tasks. Because the various parties in this setting were involved in a pro bono service, a contract with the force of law behind it was not in effect. However, that does not mean that we did not seek a written commitment from the various parties. Called a memorandum of agreement, the document stipulated what each party would commit to the project. A designated official for each institution was asked to sign it. While there is no legal value in such a document, there is a great deal of psychological value to it. Once signed by the institutional designate, to not follow through would cause the institution to lose a great deal of credibility within the local government, other social service systems, and the public - especially when signing the memorandum was given extensive media coverage! The foregoing is particularly true when an advocacy group such as the Alliance for the Mentally Ill is providing a watchdog function.

After a series of meetings where the skeletal form of the program was laid out, there was agreement between the mental health professionals present that they would provide teaching staff for training and also coordinate their institutions in collaborating with the police once the plan was put into action. The Shelby City Alliance for the Mentally Ill, the Shelby Police Department, the local state mental hospital, community mental health clinics, the emergency psychiatric unit of the city hospital, the mayor's office, the counseling, psychology and social work departments of the state university, the psychiatric department of the medical school, and the Shelby judical district all signed the memorandum.

Physically entering the system. Because of the complexity of this program and the numerous systems that potentially interact with the violently mentally ill, it was important for the consultants to have more than name recognition or hold formal meetings. As a result, we spent a great deal of time physically going to specific

143

institutions, talking with different professionals, and studying how they functioned to better understand how the various parts could be integrated into the whole.

Psychologically entering the system. The Alliance for the Mentally Ill played a key part in our entry into the total system. Because of their advocacy role they could open political doors where we or the police department could not. Further, if we did not have their backing, they could bring that same force to bear against us! As a result, all of our organizational and planning meetings included representatives of this group.

Because consultants must earn their way into a system, a critical component of system change is obtaining credibility with those who will be asked to carry out the program. Since the consultants would be involved directly in training the officers, it was extremely important that we establish our "bona fides" with them. While our degrees and titles might get us through the door, they would not guarantee us acceptance or success. We would need to create a psychological bond with these men and women if they were to believe what we said and be willing to literally risk their lives putting our techniques into practice. Therefore, we decided that we would cross-train with the officers as would the rest of the trainers. That is, we would ride with the officers on the evening shift to learn what they faced every time a mental disturbance call came over the radio. Doing this would provide us with a wealth of practical information to use in training and word would quickly spread among the officers that we were willing to put ourselves at risk with them.

Diagnosis. Gathering Information. While local data were being gathered to substantiate the kind and degree of intervention needed, we also surveyed metropolitan police departments across the country in regard to their operational responses to mental disturbance calls. We were particularly interested in programs that could be easily replicated, were cost effective, and could provide service to thousands of mental disturbance calls a year. Once these surveys were returned, we used the data to brainstorm with the police department. While ideas we generated might be "brilliantly" conceived, it would be up to the police to carry them out. Therefore, it was extremely important that any possible intervention plan be critically appraised by the local department in regard to the plan's strategic, tactical, and logistical utility.

Defining the problem. Responses to our survey indicated that some police departments used centrally-located speciality units which were specifically trained for crisis intervention with the mentally ill. Other departments had phone linkages to mental health providers that could send crisis response teams of mental health workers to the scene. No programs were found which used what we will call a *specialist-generalist* approach. That is, using regular patrol officers as crisis interventionists who would be given specific training in calming and defusing violent situations with the mentally ill. Even though no other police department had such a program, logistically this idea seemed to have merit because it would have specialists throughout the city who could respond rapidly to calls.

Setting goals. At that point in time, the goal of the program was to create a crisis intervention team which would be specifically trained in skill areas to understand and deal with the mentally ill. These officers would be initially screened through psychological testing, interviewed from a pool of volunteers, have their performance records reviewed, and be recommended by their commanders.

Generating possible interventions. Options we considered were the use of the hostage negotiation unit (a specially trained team of crisis intervention officers housed at a central location) and teaming up police with rapid response teams from local mental health clinics. However, these options failed the two critical criteria of meeting the sheer number of calls and responding to those calls quickly. The specialist-generalist approach was still felt to have the most merit, but the major problem with it was the question of whether regular patrol officers could be trained to do this very difficult job or if we could even entice any of them into volunteering to do it.

Implementation. The first few moments when law enforcement arrives on the scene are the most critical and typically predicate whether or not the eventual outcome will be resolved peacefully. Therefore, we decided it would be too cumbersome to have centrally-located units or specialty response teams when the department averaged over 5,000 mental disturbance calls a year in a heavily populated 200 square mile area. The specialist-generalist approach which would use regular patrol officers was discussed at length with the mental health professionals and consensus was reached that carefully selected patrol officers could be trained to do the job. Our fears that we would not obtain enough volunteers were groundless. By providing a $50 per month hazardous duty pay to "sweeten" the deal, our initial request obtained over 100 volunteers.

Formulating a plan. Because training patrol officers was a vital component of the program, a great deal of effort and thought went into formulating what the specific training would entail. All of the mental health professionals who had signed the memorandum of agreement cooperated in drawing up a training program. In its final form, that program involved eighty hours of training that included the following curriculum:

* Diagnostic and clinical issues of the dangerous mentally ill
* Diagnostic and clincial issues of Posttraumatic Stress Disorder
* Basic crisis intervention techniques for controlling aggressive behavior
* Suicide intervention techniques

146

* Treatment strategies for crisis intervention
* Patient rights and legal aspects of crisis intervention
* Types, use, and side effects of psychotropic medications
* Alcohol and drug behavior in the mentally ill
* Articulation and coordination of police/caseworker roles
* Specialized training in nonlethal forms of physical containment such as the Taser electric stun device and pepper gas
* Simulation activities that include videotaped role play and critique of officer performance
* Face-to-face discussions between officers and patients at a local mental hospital about their perceptions of one another.

Two of the more important points about the training program are worthy of discussion. First, we believe that a training program should have hands-on training and be highly practical in providing skills that participants can easily acquire and use. We firmly believe that any consulting activity that involves training should demonstrate and not just talk about what it proposes its participants to do. We believe that as trainers we should model the behaviors we are asking participants in that training to perform. Simulation activities are one of the most critical components of training because they allow participants to practice in a safe place where they can laugh at one another's miscues, applaud creative responses, and learn from each other.

The other critical component of this training was arranging for officers to have face-to-face dialogues with the mentally ill. While such dialogues were extremely difficult to do because of the legal issues associated with confidentiality, they were extremely important in giving officers a perspective on the mentally ill's perception of the officer and allaying officers' fears of "crazy" people. To solve this problem, each officer signed an agreement

147

not to disclose any information or reveal the identities of patients they met during training.

Immediately after training was completed, along with the police lieutenant and captain who were responsible for the crisis intervention officers' supervision, we debriefed all trainers. Besides reviewing written and verbal evaluations of the participants, we also discussed the specific components of training, how they were sequenced, and what we might change, add, or delete.

Once training was completed we had 95 trained specialist-generalist crisis intervention officers available for duty. These officers were placed on duty rosters that would put them in all precincts on all three shifts. This distribution would allow dispatchers to call a crisis intervention officer to respond to a mental disturbance call within minutes in any part of the city.

Evaluating the plan. To monitor the effectiveness of training we decided to have all trainers ride with crisis intervention officers as soon after start-up as it was feasible for them to do so. We also committed to have monthly update sessions with the crisis team supervisors which would include selected mental health professionals who had helped in training. The purpose of these meetings was to trouble shoot the plan and evaluate it for any shortcomings. After four months into the program we concluded the following:

    1.   Many officers had performed exceedingly well, but there was no vehicle to apprise them of that fact other than word of mouth. That is an exceedingly poor communication method when officers operate on three shifts in five different precincts. Exchange of information between officers as to what worked and did not work was vital. Based upon that finding, a crisis intervention officer newsletter

detailing critical incidents was started by the supervisor.

2. As carefully as we had prepared both top level administrators and rank and file officers, we neglected first level supervisors such as lieutenants who function as field supervisors. As a result, when a crisis intervention officer made the scene of a mental disturbance call, he or she was supposed to be in charge. However, field supervisors sometimes felt their authority was being usurped, which caused conflicts at the site of the call. It became apparent that we needed to train field supervisors as quickly as possible to alleviate this problem.

3. Crisis intervention officers carried no special identification badges. At times, this lack of identification caused miscommunication. Relatives or friends seeking assistance did not know which officers to talk to, nor at times did other officers, paramedics, or other professional staff who might be on the scene of the call. It became apparent that some means of identification was needed. Therefore, a blue and silver medallion was designed which would be worn on the officer's uniform blouse and would clearly identify him or her as a crisis intervention officer. What we were unaware of was that wearing the medallion began to signify membership in an elite group. Officers started to wear them as badges of honor.

Once we learned of the pride with which these medallions were worn, we suggested that all of the trainers be given them as concrete evidence of their inclusion as equal and contributing partners with the police officers. A pinning ceremony and certification of appreciation awards ceremony was given at the police academy for all the trainers by the Mayor and the police chief. By providing the medallions to the trainers they became

149

bonded to and positively identified themselves as an integral part of the police force.

Disengagement. The acid test of consultation is whether the plan that has been formulated is meeting its goal. While reports from the general public and personal testimonals from members of the Alliance for the Mentally Ill were highly laudatory, hard data was the critical evaluation factor. A series of statistical tests was conducted on pre- and post-intervention measures over a sixteen month period. Statistically significant differences were found on increased calls, increased transportation to mental health facilities, decreased injuries to officers and the mentally ill, and decreased barricade/hostage situations. These statistics indicated that the program plan had immediate positive effects. To ascertain if the program had lasting effects, the same statistical analyses were conducted after a three year period of operation. Again, the same results were found. Perhaps most important of all, no deaths or critical injuries to a mentally ill person have occurred at the hands of the crisis intervention officers during the time the program has been in operation.

Reducing involvement and following up. Disengagement occurred by our systematically removing ourselves from involvement in the program. We do not believe that any consulting assistance should be terminated abruptedly or automatically. As staff are able to take on more and more responsibilities, many of the consultant's roles can be turned over to them. As an example, as supervisory staff become familiarized with the process and procedures and form bonds with mental health professionals, they have taken on the responsibility for setting up training and recruiting mental health professionals for it. Seven years after start-up of the program we still do one component of yearly training for new crisis intervention classes, but the day-to-day running of the program is clearly in the capable hands of veteran crisis intervention officers. However, provisions do need to be made for continuous and timely follow-up as requested. In our case, we

150

have conducted follow-up training by using incidents that crisis intervention officers have experienced to refine intervention techniques.

Terminating. Finally, successful consultation often evolves into requests for assistance with other issues within the system. For example, we still work closely with the Shelby City Police Department and have been involved in establishing a major program to combat domestic violence and are now working on a school violence project. In short, for the consultant, nothing breeds success like success!

Implications for Practice

In the human service business, clear and concrete indications that something works are often few and far between. Probably there is no better test for the consultation process or reinforcement for consultants than to see objective data that their plan or program is working and that their work is being replicated by others. That is certainly true for us. Many other police departments from around the country now send officers to Shelby City for training in crisis intervention with the mentally ill. Further, components of the crisis intervention training we were responsible for are now integrated into all recruit training at the Shelby City Police Academy.

At best, working with systems that have different perspectives and may be antagonistic towards the human service worker is difficult work for consultants. In working with such clients, consultants will need to vigorously practice empathic listening and responding skills. Likewise, it is imperative that consultants have expertise in understanding the dynamics and techniques for operating within task groups. Possessing and understanding organizational dynamics and knowing how to gain entry and move within the organization are skills critical to effectively coping with political

151

issues, the bureaucracy, and the organization's method of operation. Key to such operations are identifying group members who are open to divergent views, can articulate their own viewpoints, and can coordinate among systems. Moving these key players into leadership roles is critical when systems are paranoid about one another, many individual egos are involved, and organizational "turf" boundaries are being changed.

A consumer advocacy group group such as the Shelby City Alliance for the Mentally Ill can be a blessing and a curse! The group can be a blessing from the standpoint that they can bring a great deal of political pressure to bear on bureaucracies that no other organization or institution can. Thus, they are invaluable in helping the consultant expedite systemic change that otherwise might take years to accomplish. They may also be a curse if they are summarily dismissed as "agitators who know litttle of the reality of the situation." If they are not carefully involved and given recognition for the critical part they play in making systemic change, that same pressure can be brought to bear on the consultants!

A valuable asset in this consultation was the commitment and involvement of the administration of the Shelby City Police Force. Consultants should strongly consider avoiding an organization that is not willing to have its top administration committed to and involved in training, program development, and evaluation. Unless the policy makers of an organization are personally involved in the training and professional development of rank and file personnel, they are de facto implying that the training is not worth their time and effort. That message is implicitly carried to employees who are then likely to be less than enthusiatic about changes they are asked to make. Further, if policy makers are not involved in training and feedback they will be less aware of the scope and depth of knowledge and competency that their employees have gained. Lack of understanding of the employees' new skills and limits of those skills can have serious implications as those skills are carried into practice in the real world.

Perhaps the most potent result of administrative involvement in the system consultation process is the benefit of multidisciplinary thinking when different systems are brought together. A key element in consultation with multiple systems is that people and ideas from different disciplines, perspectives, cultural, and training backgrounds enhance and broaden administrative thinking. Such paradigmatic shifts are not easy for traditionally conservative systems such as police departments and some mental health agencies to make. Therefore, it is important to slowly and patiently bring such diverse systems together while reinforcing them and continuously pointing out the benefits of doing so.

We would add in closing that one of the most serious mistakes consultants can make is not being willing to model what they are doing. Talking about problems and their theoretical implications is fine, but what most consultees want are clear action plans and models to solve what are for them unsolvable problems. The best way we know how to do that is to show the consultee what we are talking about by demonstrating it.

An example is our modeling "verbal de-escalating, defusing, and calming techniques" with trainees in subsequent training sessions after the crisis intervention team went into operation. During Friday evening shifts the consultants rode with different crisis intervention officers who were identified by their supervisors as highly competent. The consultants and their accompanying crisis intervention officers collaborated on constructing several written training scenarios directly from crisis situations the officers and consultants had encountered. The consultants and the crisis intervention officers modeled appropriate crisis intervention techniques by reenacting these scenarios and then processing with the trainees what they had done and why they did it. We then used similar scenarios where trainees were required to deal with emergent and realistic crises and were videotaped while doing so. These videotapes were then played back in the training room and critiqued by both consultants and experienced crisis intervention officers. By using these experienced officers and also subjecting ourselves to critical review, we established program credibility and our own credibility, and provided an atmosphere that was conducive for trainees to try out their skills. Thus, this example correctly depicts consultants as being richly involved <u>with</u> consultees rather than doing something <u>for</u> them.

References and Suggested Readings

Dougherty, A. M. (1995). <u>Consultation: Practice and perspectives in school and community settings</u>. (2nd ed.). Pacific Grove, CA: Brooks/Cole. (Chapter 9).

Gilliland, B. E., & James, R. K. (1993). <u>Crisis intervention strategies.</u> (2nd ed.). Pacific Grove, CA: Brooks-Cole. (Chapter 13).

Hansen, J.C., Himes, B.S., & Meier, S. (1990). <u>Consultation: Concepts and practices</u>. Englewood Cliffs, NJ: Prentice-Hall, Inc. (Chapter 8).

Editor's Note: Now that you have read this case, reflect upon it and develop a list of five things you might have done differently if you were a consultant involved with the case.

CHAPTER NINE

MENTAL HEALTH CASE CONSULTATION

Frances E. Tack and Lynn Hayes

Setting and Background Issues

<u>Setting</u>. This mental health consultation case explores the death and dying issues associated with counseling people with AIDS and the behavioral inconsistencies inherent in the transition from living to dying. The consultation resulted from a case at a local AIDS service organization in a medium-sized southeastern city. This community-based, non-profit agency employees a total of twelve full- and part-time employees and utilizes over 150 volunteers to provide a range of services to people with HIV/AIDS, their families and care-givers.

This AIDS service organization was founded several years ago, beginning as a board of directors without provisions for services, space or clients. Through community networking and commitment, it has grown into one of the premier not-for-profit agencies in the city. It provides comprehensive needs assessment, counseling, financial assistance, resource coordination, and care giving services. (Editor's note: For a thorough discussion on establishing AIDS education programs, see House & Walker, 1993). The agency now occupies its own space and has over 200 active clients at any given time from as many as seventeen counties. About a quarter of the agency's clients die each year.

The organization has wrestled with many of the issues common to AIDS service organizations: confidentiality, the duty to warn, employee/volunteer burnout, organizational turnover, and the numerous medical advances in the treatment of HIV/AIDS. (Editor's note: See Keeling (1993) for a review of medical advances related to AIDS). Of these, employee/volunteer burnout and organizational turnover have been the most chronic due to the high stress of working with terminal patients with a socially stigmatized disease. As a counselor, it is hard to see clients die and it is hard to see society reject and blame those with the disease. For these reasons, the AIDS service organization has become sensitized to the need for and has developed policy in support of employee/volunteer counseling, consultation, extended holidays and day-to-day grief support.

Background. Some general background on working with people with HIV/AIDS is important to set the stage for the case and to understand some of the underlying issues associated with consultation and counseling related to this population.

First is the issue of confronting death and dying. Primary here is assisting the client in confronting death and working through unresolved issues which are blocking the emotional progress toward acceptance. Consultation can be a means of exploring such techniques a counselor can use to facilitate the client in this process. Also, inherent in working with terminal clients (but not always conscious for us) is the fear and contemplation of our own eventual deaths. As will be described, in this case I helped the consultee become aware of some of her own issues about death and made a subsequent counseling referral for her.

Next, as I approached this case, it was critical for me to keep in mind the social stigmatization of people with HIV/AIDS and the dynamics this can set up for the counselor/client relationship and the consultant/consultee relationship. As Dworkin and Pincu (1993) discuss, there is an array of issues, including homosexuality, drug abuse, and sexism, which has led to the stigmatization of people with AIDS. Going into the consultation, it was important for me to be clear about my personal values on these issues and be prepared to be open and non-judgmental. It was also important for me to listen for these themes in the consultation which might give clues to some of the dynamics between the counselor and the client.

The particular case which led to the consultation involved a thirty-eight year old gay male with AIDS. This client and his life partner of ten years had been clients of the agency for approximately two years. During this time, the client had received counseling services from one AIDS service organization staff member who had been assigned to the case from the client's first contact with the agency.

The counselor had felt comfortable with the progress of the counseling until a few months prior to the consultation, when the client's physical health deteriorated rapidly and the progress of the counseling stalled. The counselor was at a loss as to how to emotionally assist this particular client through the next phases of the dying process and recognized her need for consultation on death and dying issues.

Consultation Goals

The general goals of the consultation with this consultee (the AIDS service organization counselor) involved facilitating the consultee's knowledge of and comfort with the topic of death and exploring ways for the consultee to assist her client with the same issues. The consultee expressed a need for more information on the stages of emotional response that a dying client experiences. Further, the consultee expressed to me her interest in expanding her repertoire of techniques and approaches in working with terminal clients.

It also quickly became clear that the consultee had some personal issues with death and some boundary issues about how much to give the client and when to say "no." Therefore, it was also a goal of the consultation to assist the consultee in outlining a self-care and support plan. The consultee was interested in both personal and professional self-care plans. That is, she wanted to develop a better stress management plan for herself and explore her own issues with death and dying, while at the same time clarifying her professional boundaries with clients and defining the level of interaction she could give to this particular client on a routine basis.

Consultant Function and Roles

This consultation required me to take on several roles, including listener, expert, teacher, facilitator, and advisor. Initially, listening and facilitating the consultee through clearly defining her concerns and goals was central. Following that, my primary role for the remainder of the consultation was more of an expert and teacher on the topic of death and dying. It was this phase where we focused the bulk of our attention and for which the consultee had specifically sought me out as a consultant. In the role of advisor, I clarified and reflected the consultee's personal issues with death and suggested or "advised" a course of action, that being referral for personal counseling.

Due to the complexity and sensitivity of the issues, the case required me as consultant to utilize strong process skills to facilitate the consultee through clarifying her needs and concerns and defining goals. It was also my responsibility to structure the sessions and plan and processes which would lead to meeting the consultee's goals.

Consultee's Experience in Consultation

The consultee's primary roles in the consultation were of student and collaborator. The consultee had identified the need to learn more about the death and dying process, and we identified two routes to accomplish this:

1. Training provided by the consultant and
2. Continuing education/professional development.

In this role of student, the consultee took notes and asked questions during my delivery of training and generally interacted with me as she would a teacher. For example, when discussing the emotional stages that a terminal client goes through, I explained concepts using a flip chart and the consultee participated by asking for clarification, making connections related to her client, and taking notes.

The consultee acted as a collaborator by equally contributing with me in the definition of needs, goals and plans. The consultee also collaborated in the development of specific interventions and the plan of interaction with the client. Though I acted as an educator, giving information to the consultee (including suggesting various techniques), we worked together in tailoring the approaches we developed to fit the specific needs of her client. It is important to remember that, generally speaking, the consultee knows the client better than the consultant does. In fact, the consultant generally does not know the client at all. Therefore, the consultee is the prime source of information for the tailoring of various approaches for that client.

159

Application: Consultant Techniques and Procedures

Entry. During the initial session, I listened actively as the consultee described the case and her concerns. I probed for additional information concerning the progression of the disease and the client's reactions at various stages. The consultee shared the case with me, including her concerns about the client and her interest in gaining some additional insight about death and dying. She explained the focus of the counseling with the client over the past two years and particularly the last six months.

Though living with full blown AIDS, the client was generally healthy and the counselor felt comfortable with the progress of the counseling. However, six months prior to the consultation, the client's health began declining and continued to decline for four months, culminating in the client acquiring a debilitating, opportunistic infection. The onset of the infection caused the client to become bedridden, devastating the client and pushing the client to another level in terms of facing death.

At this point, the counselor's focus shifted to helping the client adjust to the physical changes in his life and to process the frustration, anger and grief that he was experiencing. It was during this stage of the counseling that the client began to demonstrate naturally contradictory behavior related to death. He would be wishing to die and concerned about funeral arrangements one minute, saying he didn't want his partner to have to deal with that after his death. The next minute, he would be concerned about whether his lunch would be delivered on time and who was going to clean the house. After pursuing these issues with the client for two months, the counselor felt that the client's progress had stalled, and the counselor was unsure where to go from here. Though having worked with dying clients previously, the counselor felt that the client's history and strong mixed messages (e.g., not taking medications vs. worrying about nutritional content of meals) created a situation for which the counselor needed consultation

160

relative to the issues of counseling dying clients. It was at this point, the consultee explained, that she sought consultation from me, selecting me due to my role as a counselor with the local Hospice organization.

The consultee discussed her general concerns about assisting the client through the stages of dying and expressed concern over her client refusing the take his physician-prescribed medications. The consultee saw this refusal as another aspect of the confusion the client was experiencing related to accepting versus denying death. The client expressed a continuing desire to fight the disease and live, yet refused his medications because of his fear they would just prolong a low quality existence.

Diagnosis. The second session was focused on specifically defining the areas of concern and establishing goals for the consultation which would meet the needs the consultee had outlined. As the consultee expressed her concerns and needs, I recorded them on poster paper. After having discussed all of her concerns, I facilitated the consultee through combining similar concerns and prioritizing them. Then, through discussion and brainstorming, we established four goals for the consultation:

1. defining interventions to help the consultee facilitate the client in decision making about moving into the death process and reconciling with his death;
2. exploring ways for the consultee to facilitate the client's grief process concerning multiple losses leading up to death and death itself;
3. providing the consultee with information on death and dying and identifying sources for further training and professional development; and
4. defining a plan of action for the counselor to take care of herself while assisting the client through the death process.

161

In delineating these goals, the consultee and I recognized that goals one and two overlapped and were not necessarily separable. Nevertheless, we felt it important to be specific about the objectives of consultation and the concerns the consultee had about the client.

Implementation. The client identified that her highest priority was gaining additional information; therefore, in session three, I shared information with the consultee in a didactic manner, providing resources to the consultee and teaching the consultee the basics of the death process from spiritual, emotional, cognitive, behavioral and physical perspectives.

Since I worked primarily with dying clients and had access to many resources, I compiled a resource list for the consultee consisting of books, professional organizations, and training opportunities (workshops, seminars, conferences, etc.). I reviewed this with the consultee and together we generated a plan of specific resources the consultee would pursue and when she would pursue them. The consultee decided that two of the books, one dealing with death and dying and the other on the physical progression of AIDS, seemed especially appropriate and decided to read those immediately. One seminar on death and dying and one AIDS conference were also identified and the consultee planned to check with her supervisor on getting time off from work to attend these.

I explained to the consultee what she could expect in terms of the spiritual issues which may arise for the client, the different feelings the client might experience, the effect dying has on belief systems, things her client might do and say, and the physical progression of a body which is dying.

In session four, I shared case examples from my own experience, suggested interventions, and discussed various counseling approaches with the consultee. Specifically, I suggested the use of the following techniques:

1. facilitating the client's guided visualization of the dying experience;
2. challenging the client to list all unfinished business and fears of death;
3. encouraging the client to engage in dialogue with his body to understand what, if anything, his body is telling him.

With this base, we developed a plan of action for the consultee to try with the client over two sessions. This plan recognized the fact that the actual process of the consultee facilitating the client through the transition from living to dying and working through grief issues could not be accomplished in two sessions and actually would continue in some form until the client's death. The intention of the two-session approach was for the consultee to try out some new strategies, discuss the client's responses to those strategies with me, and to adjust the strategies as necessary.

Also in session four, I pursued issues related to goal four, that of the consultee taking care of herself while assisting her client through the death process. During this discussion, the consultee spoke of her own grief issues associated with this client and the need she felt for personal support. She also mentioned her own fear of death and concern that this could get in the way of her working with her client on death and dying issues.

In response to these concerns, the consultee and I brainstormed ways in which the consultee could take care of herself while working with this client. The list was narrowed down and prioritized, and a plan was developed. The consultee decided to spend no more than two hours per week with this client, to plan one fun outing for herself per week, to discuss this case regularly with her supervisor, and to seek support as needed from the other agency staff members. In addition, since the consultee had some personal issues she wanted to deal with surrounding death, I suggested that the consultee seek personal counseling and referred her to a counselor experienced in this area.

In total, we developed three plans:

1. one concerning counseling strategies to address goals one and two;
2. another which was a consultee professional development plan to address goal three; and
3. a third consisting of a consultee self-care plan to address goal four.

In session five, the consultee shared with me her progress on the three plans. Specifically, she explained the interventions and approaches she had used with her client over the two counseling sessions she had conducted with him since last meeting with me. The consultee shared that the guided visualization had helped her client pinpoint his fears about death and helped him realize that he wasn't ready to die, but rather was depressed about his suffering and immobility. The consultee also indicated that the process of listing unfinished business had been very powerful for her client. Through this exercise he had discovered that he has quite a bit of living left to do and finally decided to start taking the medication that he had previously refused.

The consultee generally felt that the changes in her approach had been helpful though she questioned her client's readiness for having a dialogue with his body and decided to wait on this approach until he seemed more ready. Overall, she felt that the listing of unfinished business had been the most fruitful in helping the client sort through the mixed feelings of wanting to live and wanting to die.

The consultee also discussed her progress on implementing the professional development plan which had been established in session three and the self-care plan which had been established in session four. Specifically, the consultee had acquired both of the recommended books and had begun reading the one on death. Her supervisor had agreed to give her time off to attend the seminar, but felt that five days away from work for her to attend the week–long conference during that particular month would put too big of a strain on the agency. The supervisor had agreed that she could attend a workshop or seminar on AIDS instead, so we selected one from the resource which would suffice in lieu of the conference.

Lastly, the consultee reported on her self–care plan, indicating that she had done fairly well, but would have to put specific energy into setting clearer boundaries concerning time spent with the client. She had planned and done her fun outings, discussed the case with her supervisor, and sought out support from her peers at the agency. However, the consultee reported having spent four hours one week with the client, which went beyond the target of two hours she had established. She felt this had drained her substantially and had probably hampered the services she provided to other clients later that day and the next day. With my facilitation, the consultee explored this issue further and decided to be more specific with the client when scheduling sessions, indicating to him that, barring unforeseen emergencies, the sessions would need to end as planned. In addition, she planned in her next session with the client to openly discuss her need to take care of herself so she could provide the best service possible to him.

Disengagement. At the end of session five, it appeared to both the consultee and me that the original goals of the consultation had been accomplished. At this point, I checked in with the consultee to be sure that there were no additional goals which may have arisen throughout the course of the consultation which needed to be addressed. The consultee indicated that she felt she needed time to digest the new information and continue to apply the new approaches they had developed before she tackled any other issues with this case. Therefore, having reached the goals of the consultation, we scheduled a final session in which to discuss the consultation and reach closure.

In this final session, I solicited the consultee for feedback concerning the consultation. Though having worked with dying patients and having been somewhat familiar with the death process, the consultee indicated that the instruction received from me was very helpful, and that seeing all the aspects presented holistically gave her a new perspective on death. Through the exercise she was able to pinpoint specifically where her client was in relation to spirituality, feelings, thoughts, behaviors, and physical decline and to more appropriately utilize various techniques and interventions. The consultee indicated that this information would allow her to be more aware of what her client was going through and help the client to teach his life partner and other family members about the process.

The consultee also expressed appreciation for now having her own professional development and self–care plans. These were areas which she had wanted to focus on but just had not found the time to plan. She particularly felt that seeking her own personal counseling had already had a big impact on her and was something she planned to continue for several months.

Implications for Practice

A mental health consultation case such as this one provides many lessons about providing positive consultation and the consultant skills needed to accomplish the goals of consultation. First, it is important to recognize that even an experienced counselor may need consultation. In this case, the consultee had been working with terminally ill clients and had faced the issues of death and dying many times; however, this particular client provided some unique challenges which pushed the counselor into unknown territory, a situation which the counselor healthily recognized and sought to remedy. Minimizing or shaming of the consultee by me as the consultant when presented with an experienced counselor who "should already know this" could have been very damaging to the counselor's self–esteem and ultimately to the services rendered to the client. Instead, my openness and validation of the consultee's needs encouraged her to be clear about the deficits and fostered a trusting, collaborative relationship.

Second, this case makes clear the issue of me knowing myself as a consultant; that is, recognizing my own issues, limits and areas of expertise. In this case, if I had not been an expert on death and dying issues, but had tried to "fake it" with the consultee, I would not only have unethically misrepresented myself, but also would not have been able to adequately assist the consultee in accomplishing her goals related to gaining more information. If I found that her need to learn about the dying process was beyond my limits of expertise or if other issues which I could not handle had arisen, it would have been imperative for me to have referred her to another consultant.

This case demonstrates some of the sensitive issues a consultant might be exposed to, including AIDS, death and homosexuality, and drives home the need for consultants to be clear about their own values and seek personal counseling where necessary to work on these issues. As Dworkin and Pincu (1993) express, issues such as gay and lesbian lifestyles, the inevitable death of clients, and the unpredictable nature of AIDS can be overwhelming and complex. In terms of process, it is important to recognize that sensitive issues may also extend the entry phase. The consultee and consultant may need more time to build their relationship and build trust prior to the consultee feeling comfortable discussing certain topics or sharing certain needs.

This case highlights the importance of strong consultant process skills. Many cases, including this one, involve complicated scenarios, overlapping issues and needs, and a confusion of

167

possibilities. This was why the consultee came to me for consultation. Strong consultant process skills help the consultee sort out these issues, make sense of them, and put them in perspective. Once this is accomplished, goal setting and plans of action become much easier. The primary process skills used in this case included

1.   active listening and clarification,
2.   drawing connections, and
3.   brainstorming, combining and prioritizing.

I should also address the grey area that the consultee and I entered when we developed the consultee's self–care plans. As we know, consultation is about working with a consultee on a work–related case involving a third party (the client). Consultation is not counseling for the consultee. As such, the fact that we developed the consultee's self–care plan during the consultation put us in a sort of grey area: the plan was critical to the consultee's effectiveness with this particular client, but at the same time was somewhat of a broad personal issue. In this case, I made a judgment as we moved into this phase of the consultation that a high–level self–care plan coupled with a counseling referral for the consultee was an appropriate consultative response to the concerns raised. Though the development of the self–care plan could be construed as counseling, the clear boundaries and open attitude of the consultee led me to believe this positive step could be taken in a reasonable amount of time and could provide immediate strategies for the consultee without getting into the depths of counseling type issues. In another case with a different consultee, I might not have made the same judgment.

Another implication for consideration is the appropriate number of sessions for a mental health consultation. This case involved six sessions over a two month period, somewhat long for a case of this type. This is where being clear about the boundaries between consultation and counseling are critical so that the consultee's time

168

is truly spent receiving case consultation. In addition, the consultant needs to be aware of the consultee's needs and agenda. In this scenario, the consultee had a clear vision of her needs and was quite motivated to pursue a wide range of goals related to her case. Had this not been the situation, I might have suggested a less aggressive list of goals initially, conducted the consultation in two to three sessions, and invited the consultee to return at some later date to pursue other aspects of the case.

References and Suggested Readings

Caplan, G. (1977). Mental health consultation: Retrospect and prospect. In S. C. Plog & P. I. Ahmed (Eds.), Principles and techniques of mental health consultation (pp. 9–21). New York: Plenum.

Caplan, G., & Caplan, R. B. (1993). Mental health consultation and collaboration. San Francisco: Jossey–Bass. (Chapters 6 and 7).

Corey, G., Corey, M. S., & Callanan, P. (1993). Issues and ethics in the helping professions. (4th ed.). Pacific Grove, CA: Brooks/Cole. (Chapter 11).

Dougherty, A. M. (1995). Consultation : Practice and perspectives in school and community settings. (2nd ed.). Pacific Grove, CA: Brooks/Cole. (Chapter 10).

Dworkin, S. H., & Pincu, L. (1993). Counseling in the era of AIDS. Journal of Counseling & Development, 71, 275–281.

Herlihy, B., & Corey, G. (1992). Dual relationships in counseling. Alexandria, VA: American Association for Counseling and Development.

House, R. M., & Walker, C. M. (1993). Preventing AIDS via education. Journal of Counseling & Development, 71, 282–289.

Keeling, R. P. (1993). HIV disease: Current concepts. Journal of Counseling & Development, 71, 261–274.

Werner, J. L., & Tyler, J. M. (1993). Community–based interventions: A return to community mental health centers' origins. <u>Journal of Counseling & Development,</u> <u>71</u>, 689–692.

Editor's Note: Now that you have read this case, reflect upon it and develop a list of five things you might have done differently if you were a consultant involved with the case.

CHAPTER TEN

CONCLUSIONS

A. Michael Dougherty

This brief chapter pulls together some of the main ideas that run through the cases which comprise Chapters 2 through 9. Since each of these chapters has an "Implications for Practice" section, I will focus on some general issues and concepts about human services consultation that the cases point to. These issues and concepts are discussed under the following headings:

* Consultation Is First and Foremost a Human Relationship
* The Personal Characteristics of the Consultant Are Most Likely a Critical Factor Related to Consultation Success
* The Consultee Should Be Recognized as a Valuable Asset in the Consultation Process
* All Consultation Occurs in Some Organizational Context
* Consultation Has Many Common Sense Elements
* Consultation Is a Developmental Process

*   The "How" of Consultation Is as Important as the "What"

Consultation Is First and Foremost a Human Relationship

Human service consultants do not consult *to* their consultees but rather they consult *with* them. When consultation is viewed as a human relationship, its personal side becomes as important as its professional side. Since consultation is a relationship among humans, it needs to be conducted with a personal touch. Many of the authors of the cases pointed to the importance of the human side of consultation. Carrington Rotto notes the importance of integrating positive interpersonal skills with technical expertise to maximize consultant-consultee effectiveness. Deck and Isenhour as well as James, Crews and Gilliland point to the importance of consultants modeling the very behaviors they want their consultees to acquire. Such "walking the talk" demonstrates the consultant's trust in him- or herself and at the same time also shows the consultant's humanness. Such modeling also provides the atmosphere in which consultees are more willing to try out new behaviors. Tack and Hayes reflect a different aspect of the human side of the consultation relationship when they point out the difficulty in differentiating between a counseling and a consultation relationship. When they discuss the self-care plan with which the consultant assisted the consultee, did this focus on the consultee constitute a counseling relationship? Or was it simply helping the consultee make a plan that would effectively benefit the consultee and her future clients? The answer to these questions are not clear, particularly in light of the fact that the consultant had referred the consultee to a counselor. The bottom line is, because consultation is an interpersonal relationship in which all parties have the opportunity to benefit, consultants need to be responsive to the human side of consultation if consultation is to be successful (Henning-Stout, 1994; Dougherty, 1995).

The Personal Characteristics of the Consultant Are Most Likely a Critical Factor Related to Consultation Success

Part of the conventional wisdom of consultation is that the personal characteristics of consultants are a critical factor in the success of consultation. Several of the authors pointed out the importance of the personal characteristics of consultants. Carlson points out the importance of consultants being risk takers. Tack and Dougherty note the importance of objectivity as it relates to the consultant's work. These same authors point out the importance of the quality of openness to feedback on the part of consultants. Tack and Hayes suggest that it is very important for consultants to recognize their own issues, limits and areas of expertise. These same authors say that it is imperative that consultants be clear about their own personal values. Deck and Isenhour as well as James, Crews and Gilliland suggest the importance of genuineness on the part of the consultant. Clearly, consultants need to possess a relatively high level of self awareness to effectively conduct consultation.

The Consultee Should Be Recognized as a Valuable Asset in the Consultation Process

Consultants do not operate in a vacuum in the consultation relationship. They are influenced directly by the consultee and indirectly by the client system. Consultants can use the consultee as a resource in the consultation process and probably should do so. Golden as well as Carrington Rotto point out the importance of involving parents and teachers as resource people in working with children. Deck and Isenhour point out the importance of acknowledging the professionalism and expertise of adult learners and suggest that it is presumptuous to ignore the training and background of consultees. James, Crews and Gilliland dramatically illustrate this point when they describe riding with their police consultees on Friday evening shifts. Tack and

173

Dougherty note the importance of consultants having their consultees "be the teacher" so that the consultant can do an even better job of consulting. Becker-Reems suggests that consultants take time during the consultation process and discuss what they are learning with their consultees so as to maximize learning in the consultee and increase the probability of success in consultation. The authors of each case either directly or indirectly emphasize the importance of collaboration. Indeed, consultants seem to be well advised to take on roles, when appropriate, which maximize the use of consultees in the consultation process.

All Consultation Occurs in Some Organizational Context

The organizations in which consultation occurs have powerful forces that influence the consultation process. "Smart" consultants take these forces into consideration when providing services. Carlson, at a very basic level, points out the importance of changing the family system as a way of helping a child (in this case the client system). James, Crews and Gilliland note the importance of having the top administrators of the organization committed to and involved in the consultation process. Tack and Dougherty suggest the helpfulness of knowledge of the system in which consultation is occurring. Consultants will want to bear in mind that there are a variety of forces in organizations of any kind, such as the organization's culture, that influence the nature of consultation. By taking these forces into account the consultant and other parties are better able to utilize them to affect success in consultation.

Consultation Has Many Common Sense Elements

In consultation, "the magic is there is no magic!" Like most other enterprises, successful consultation is a combination of effective planning and hard work. Human services consultation has many common sense aspects. James, Crews and Gilliland note the importance of the consultant's interpersonal and communication skills. Golden points out that consultation is typically brief and voluntary for the parties involved. He also makes a related point: effective planning will maximize the benefit received from consultation. Deck and Isenhour echo this point in discussing their case. Carrington Rotto corroborates this same point when she emphasizes the problem-solving nature of consultation. Golden emphasizes the importance of collaboration as a way to maximize consultee input and enhance the probability of the consultee's "buying in" to the process. Golden further suggests that consultees clearly understand the "payoffs" for participating and how they relate to the "costs" in consultation as a way to have consultees invest themselves in the process. Carrington Rotto points to the importance of collaborating as a way to take into account the broader behavioral relationships across environments. Carlson recommends a thorough understanding of the presenting problem so that a well founded plan can be forged.

Deck and Isenhour as well as Carrington Rotto advocate the importance of formative evaluation. Many consultants do not evaluate their work in any manner. This is ethically questionable. Deck and Isenhour show that formative evaluation can be a useful tool to assist consultants in "staying on track" in the consultation relationship. James, Crews, and Gilliland make a strong case for the importance of summative evaluation of the consultation process. Carrington Rotto points to the importance of a relatively sophisticated evaluation design as a critical aspect of consultation. This same author also demonstrates the importance of proper assessment. Tack and Dougherty suggest that consultants point out to their consultees how they (the consultants) feel that the consultation could have been improved. Tack and Dougherty suggest that such an approach enhances the perceived genuineness of the consultant and models a non-defensive attitude for the consultee.

Tack and Dougherty highlight the notion of what parties-at-interest to involve at the preliminary exploration of organizational needs phase. They infer that all parties-at-interest should be included in the preliminary phases of consultation as a safeguard against misunderstanding and confused expectations. Further, as Becker-Reems suggests, some parties-at-interest may well become consultees in the future.

Tack and Hayes point out the obvious yet often unspoken understanding: even an *experienced* professional or parent can benefit from consultation. These same authors raise the issue of the difficulty in determining the appropriate number of sessions comprising a typical consultation relationship.

One conclusion we can draw is that in spite of its complexity, its difficulty in being defined and the permeability of its boundaries, consultation still involves many common sense elements.

Consultation Is a Developmental Process

As noted in Chapter One, consultation goes through some rather distinct stages and phases, each of which builds upon the others. Disengagement builds upon what has transpired before just as implementation builds upon entry and diagnosis. The upshot of this point is that consultants should bear this in mind when they are providing services. Consultants will want to avoid "cart before the horse" behaviors such as jumping into interventions before adequately defining the problem or moving into problem definition prior to building rapport. Some of the authors of the cases commented on the developmental nature of consultation. For example, Golden shows how setting clear expectations at the outset of consultation concerning what consultation can and cannot accomplish sets the stage for the moving into developing a contract. Carlson shows how assessment logically follows the use of interventions when he describes how relatively simple interventions can have important systemic effect. Carrington Rotto demonstrates how consultation stages build upon one another.

Becker-Reems points to the importance of marketing consultation services prior to engaging in consultation. Such marketing not only publicizes the availability of the consultant, but also helps prospective consultees grasp the essence of consultation. In addition, Becker-Reems vividly illustrates how data gathering is an essential prerequisite for defining the problem.

The "How" of Consultation Is as Important as the "What"

It's not only "what" consultants do, but also "how" they do it that is essential. That is, *how* something is done can be as important as *what* is done. For example, how a consultant and consultee communicate is as important as what they are communicating about. James, Crews and Gilliland demonstrate the importance of the consultant's ability to process the group dynamics occurring within a group of consultees. This ability to process the dynamics occurring in groups is related to effective entry and coping with issues such as organizational politics during the consultation process. Tack and Dougherty stress the importance of strong process skills on the part of the consultant. By knowing how things are going as well as what is going on, consultants are in a position to make comments on the process at any point in a consultation session. By calling attention to process issues such as how a consultee is discussing a client, consultants may shed additional light on important issues related to consultation success.

In summary, the cases in this text, show how "real life" consultation operates. You have been provided with a broad spectrum of cases so that you can see the types of activities that can be viewed as consultation. Although the consultants in the cases worked in a variety of settings and dealt with a diversity of consultees about very different problems and concerns, we could still see many commonalities in their approaches to consultation.

There are two methods by which we can expand the knowledge base in consultation. One way is through empirical research. The other is through the experiences of practicing consultants. This text and its contents are an attempt to employ the latter method.

References and Suggested Readings

Bellman, G. M. (1990). The consultant's calling: Bringing who you are to what you do. San Francisco: Jossey-Bass.

Block, P. (1981). Flawless consulting. San Diego, CA: University Associates.

Dougherty, A. M. (1995). Consultation: Practice and perspectives in school and community settings. Pacific Grove, CA: Brooks/Cole. (Chapter 2).

Henning-Stout, M. (1994). Consultation and connected knowing: What we know is determined by the questions we ask. Journal of Educational and Psychological Consultation, 5, 5-21.

Herlihy, B., & Corey, G. (1992). Dual relationships in counseling. Alexandria, VA: American Association for Counseling and Development. (Chapter 11).

Ross, G. J. (1993). Peter Block's flawless consulting and the homunculus theory: Within each person is a perfect consultant. Journal of Counseling and Development, 71, 639-641.

CHAPTER ELEVEN

CASES FOR FURTHER PRACTICE

A. Michael Dougherty

This chapter provides you with eight brief cases which allow you to apply some of the concepts of consultation to life-like situations. I have deliberately designed the cases to include dilemmas that have no "pat" answers. The idea here is to think through the cases and challenge yourself in determining how you might proceed in managing each of them. The ideas you have gleaned from your reading of the other cases in this text should provide you with a wealth of questions and strategies to use in dealing with the cases that follow. For each case, be sure to pay special attention to the information given in the section entitled "Information For Your Use In Determining How To Proceed."

Case One: A Member of a University Counseling Center Consults with the University's Director of Student Development

The Director of Student Development of a medium-sized university has sought out consultation because of increasing conflict among several of the university's fraternities. She reports that some fraternities have taken it upon themselves to "crash" other fraternities' parties. This type of behavior has led to physical violence among members of several fraternities. The director reports that there has also been some conflict among fraternities that she believes is racial in nature. Many students have reported their fear of walking or biking down "Greek Street" for fear of being accosted or caught in the middle of some conflict. The director reports that she is considering placing several of the fraternities on disciplinary probation but would like to try something as a last resort to create some positive momentum for getting the problems solved in a constructive manner. She asks the consultant to help her determine how to proceed.

Information For Your Use In Determining How To Proceed

1. The consultant is a graduate of a private university that did not permit fraternities.
2. Neither the consultant nor the director are people of color.
3. The director is actively seeking a position at another university.
4. The counseling center does not actively encourage its staff to engage in consultation.
5. There are four weeks left until the end of the academic year.

Given the information above, how might you proceed with this case?

Case Two: A Member of A University Counseling Center Consults with A Faculty Member Who Sponsors A Sorority

A faulty member who sponsors a sorority at a prestigious liberal arts college has requested consultation from one of the two counselors assigned to the school's counseling and psychological services center. During their first meeting the sponsor laments the shallow and glib image of the sorority in the eyes of many on the campus. She relates that the president of the institution has mentioned to some of the sponsor's friends that the sorority is not living up to the institution's standards of excellence. She notes that the typical grade point averages of the sisters of her sorority are significantly lower than those of other sororities. The sponsor notes that during rushes the sisters go after those students whom they think will be great "partiers." At the same time, the sponsor notes that her sorority is among the top of the Greek organizations in engaging in philanthropic efforts. The sponsor wants to enhance the image of the sorority in the eyes of the campus community as well as those of the members themselves.

Information For Your Use In Determining How To Proceed

1. The officers of the sorority are pleased with the way things are going. They don't believe the sorority has an "image problem."
2. The faculty member has been sponsoring the sorority for the past twelve years and frequently teaches honors courses.
3. There has been a history of tension between the sponsor and the various officers of the sorority over the years.
4. The sponsor gets credit for sponsoring the sorority through a stipend and "points" toward providing service to the institution.

5.   The consultant has a daughter who is a member of a
      sorority at a nearby state university. The daughter
      is on academic probation.

Given this information, how might you proceed with this case?

Case Three: A Human Services Consultant Consults with A Mid-Level Manager In An Industrial Setting

A mid-level manager in a tire manufacturing plant has contacted a human services consultant in private practice. As part of its "total quality" emphasis, the company is involved in enhancing "bottom-up" communication within the organization. The manager reports that this emphasis is backfiring in the unit for which he is responsible. He notes that the line supervisors charged with being conduits in the information flow to the manager are "distorting" the information provided by their subordinates to gain more power for themselves in the manager's unit. For example, the manager notes that inquiries regarding flexible scheduling are distorted into demands for the supervisors to have power in granting flexible work schedules without consulting with or getting the approval of the manager. The manager suggests that the consultant take on the role of observer in a series of meetings between the manager and the line supervisors.

Information For Your Use In Determining How To Proceed

1.   The consultant and the manager are former college
      roommates.
2.   The manager is the only college graduate in the
      primarily blue collar unit.
3.   The quality management movement in the company
      has been in existence for six months. The manager

has been trained in quality management, the line supervisors have not.

4. There has been a history of substance abuse among the members of the unit.

5. There is talk of the tire company merging with a Japanese firm.

Bearing these facts in mind, how would you proceed with this case?

Case Four: An Employee Assistance Program (EAP) Coordinator Consults with A Vice President Of A Telephone Company

The vice president of a telephone company has asked the coordinator of the company's employee assistance program to help her deal with a morale problem her department is having with employees in the field. A spring tornado has recently destroyed a large number of telephone lines only a couple of months after a winter storm called the "Storm of the Century" had caused a tremendous number of lines to be repaired in extreme weather. The vice president was concerned that there was a morale problem due to a discrepancy between the managers and the field workers regarding how much stress the field workers were experiencing due to work demands. The managers were coming from the point of view that the field workers were being paid overtime and consequently, the storm was providing them another "windfall." The workers, on the other hand, saw the work demands as stretching them as thin as the last storm did and wanted more work concessions than just overtime for their efforts. The vice president said she was looking for suggestions to deal with the morale problem.

Information For Your Use In determining How To Proceed

1.   The company was currently undergoing the beginnings of reorganization. The vice president's unit was affected by the reorganization plan.
2.   Part of the reorganization included a "downsizing" plan. The EAP coordinator was aware of the downsizing plan because of his unit's likely involvement in outplacement. The vice president was not aware of the downsizing plan.
3.   The vice president was said to be looking for a new position.
4.   Workers at the company as well as those at other companies owned by the parent company had gone on strike for increased benefits five years ago.
5.   The EAP coordinator had been with the company for only two years.

Considering these facts, how would you proceed with this case?

Case Five: A School-Based Consultant Consults with a Teacher

A middle school teacher asks a school-based consultant for assistance with a boy in one of the teacher's classes. The boy's father is dying of a terminal illness. The teacher is noticing the stress that the father's illness is placing on the boy. The student's academic work has deteriorated significantly over the duration of the father's illness. It is now report card time and the student has failed in the grading period two of the subjects he takes from the teacher. The teacher is concerned about the impact of the failures on the student's psychological health. The teacher wants help in determining the type of things he can do to help the child cope with the failures as well as with his father's illness.

Information For Your Use In Determining How To Proceed

1.   The child is currently in counseling having been referred to counseling by several of his teachers and the boy is in a group for children suffering loss of any kind such as loss of their family through divorce or loss of a loved one.

2.   The teacher had lost one of his own parents through death only a year before.

3.   The boy was the fourth of seven children in his family.

4.   The academic areas in which the child failed were math and social studies.

5.   The student's family belongs to a fundamentalist religious sect which had been the subject of investigative journalism into alleged "mind control" by a national television news show.

With these facts in mind, how would you proceed with this case?

Case Six: A School-Based Consultant Consults With A Parent

Two parents approached an elementary school-based consultant regarding a child's "school reluctance." The child suffered from a fear of the impending harm to or death of his parents which was causing the child (in his parents' minds) to be reluctant about coming to school. When the child arrived at school and was left against his will by the parents, the child became very anxious during the school day. The child, the younger of two children, was a "late arrival" in the family. The older sibling was now pursuing studies at a university far from the family's home town, thus making the child in effect an only child. Both parents were psychiatrists by training and consequently they were both very insightful into their own family dynamics as well as their own "personhoods." The father termed his son's diagnosis as school reluctance whereas the mother felt that the child was definitely school phobic. The parents decided that they were too close to the situation for them to help their son with this concern. The theme of harm to his parents permeated much of the child's work and play at school.

Information For Your Use In Determining How To Proceed

1. The parents were estranged from their older child who was at college.
2. The parents worked together in a private practice setting.
3. The school-based consultant was very experienced in cases such as these but was intimidated by the credentials of the parents.
4. When he was younger, the child had been placed in three different preschool programs before the parents were satisfied with the "quality" of his setting.
5. The child would wander to the window several times during the school day reporting that he was making sure that his parents were not out in the street hurt somewhere.

With these facts in mind, how would you proceed with this case?

Case Seven: A Consultant Consults With A Therapist At A Community Mental Health Center

A psychologist is under contract to provide consultation services to counselors at a community mental health center. One of the therapists asked the consultant for assistance with a case in which she was working with a client who suffered from a terminal illness. The therapist was having difficulties because the client was using denial regarding her terminal situation. In spite of the gentle but direct encountering by the therapist of the client's denial, the client continued to use denial or resistance to maneuver the sessions in other directions. Yet, the client did ask for assistance in important areas such as managing finances and learning coping strategies for the pain she was experiencing.

Information For Your Use In Determining How To Proceed

1. The therapist had never lost a significant other in her life through death.
2. The client saw the therapy sessions as meeting some of her social needs.
3. The consultant was approaching retirement age and had dealt with several bouts with cancer.
4. The therapist did not have strong religious values, the consultant had no religious values.
5. The therapist had completed eight sessions with the client. Supervisors at the mental health center actively discouraged long term therapy.

Given the information above, how might you proceed with this case?

Case Eight: A Consultant From A Mediation Center Consults In A Social Services Agency

The mediation came about due to a conflict that emerged between a supervisor and some of the social workers in a social services agency. The supervisor was doing annual performance evaluations on the social workers with "getting paper work done" being given a much higher priority over "counseling the families whom they were assigned." The role and mission of the social services agency was not clear as to whether the focus should be case management from a paper work framework or providing direct assistance to families. The conflict had grown over the last few years and consequently there was a high turnover rate among the social workers.

Information For Your Use In Determining How To Proceed

1. The consultant from the mediation center was not familiar with any of the parties involved in the conflict.
2. The consultant has a bias for social workers actually working with families and saw paper work as a bureaucratic element that blocked the ability of workers to help families.
3. The "grapevine" suggested that the workers saw the supervisor as a real "control freak."
4. The agency existed in an economically depressed urban area.
5. The spouse of the supervisor at the social services center was a prominent area politician who was instrumental in funding the grant that created the mediation center.

Given these circumstances, how would you proceed with this case?

ABOUT THE EDITOR AND CONTRIBUTORS

The Editor

A. Michael Dougherty (Ph. D., Indiana State University) is
Professor of Counseling and Head of the Department of Human
Services at Western Carolina University in Cullowhee, North
Carolina. He is author of *Consultation: Practice and Perspectives
in School and Community Settings* (Second Edition) also published
by Brooks/Cole Publishing Company. In addition to fulfilling his
duties as department head, he teaches graduate-level courses in
consultation, theories of counseling and counseling children. He
has consulted, taught courses and made presentations in a variety
of international settings including Barbados, Colombia, Cyprus,
Germany, Great Britain, Guatemala, Honduras, Jamaica, Jordan
and El Salvador.

The Contributors

Elizabeth D. Becker-Reems is the Director of Human Resource
Development at Memorial Mission Medical Center in Asheville,
North Carolina. In this capacity, she provides organizational
development services including process consultation, training,
team development, and leadership development. She is also the
organization's coordinator for the total quality management and
customer relations programs. She is the author of *Self-Managed
Teams in Health Care*, a book scheduled to be published in the fall
of 1994 by American Hospital Publishing, Inc. Elizabeth holds a

bachelor's degree in Political Science from Michigan State University and a master's degree in Human Resource Development from Western Carolina University. She is a frequent speaker on the subjects of workforce preparedness, leadership, total quality management and work teams.

Jon Carlson, Psy. D., Ed. D., ABPP, is Distinguished Professor of Counseling and Psychology at Govenors State University, University Park, Illinois. He also works as a psychologist in private practice at the Wellness Clinic in Lake Geneva, Wisconsin, and has served as the elementary school counselor/school psychologist at the Woods School in Lake Geneva since 1978. Dr. Carlson has served as president of the International Association of Marriage and Family Counselors and editor of its publication, *The Family Journal*. Dr. Carlson is currently editor of *Individual Psychology*, the journal of the North American Society of Adlerian Psychology. He has authored over 100 articles and 16 books including *Consultation: School Mental Health Professionals as Consultants* with Don Dinkmeyer, Jr. and Don Dinkmeyer, Sr.

Pamela Carrington Rotto, Ph.D., is Assistant Professor in the Department of Educational Psychology at the University of Nebraska-Lincoln. She received her doctorate in school psychology from the University of Wisconsin-Madison in 1993. Dr. Carrington Rotto has professional experience in the schools both as a school psychologist and special education teacher. Her research interests include behavioral consultation, parent training, systems of care for children with emotional disabilities, assessment and remediation of academic skill deficits, and traumatic brain injury. Dr. Carrington Rotto has background training and experience in consultation practice, research and training. Specifically, she assisted in the coordination of a federally funded research project involving training and supervision of graduate students to serve as consultants to teachers of children with emotional disabilities. She also coordinated a federally funded research project examining the effects of a treatment program which integrated the principles and procedures of behavioral case consultation and competency-based parent training.

Walter E. Crews (M. S. in Counseling and Personnel Services, Memphis State U.) is a Major in the Memphis Police Department and is currently the Coordinator of the Office of Drug Education, Prevention and Awareness for the police force. Mr. Crews is a former Commander of the Police Hostage Negotiation Team and was chairman of the inter-agency committee that designed the first police Crisis Intervention Team. He also received funding for the Family Trouble Center - a crisis counseling office for battered spouses and their abusers. Mr. Crews has been recognized for his community service with a variety of civic awards.

Mary Deck is an Associate Professor of Counselor Education in the Department of Human Services at Western Carolina University. She holds a Ph.D. in counselor education from the University of Virginia and prior to her tenure at Western Carolina, she was on the faculty at the University of Alabama. She holds membership in the American Counseling Association, American School Counselor Association, and Association for Counselor Education and Supervision, as well as in regional and state associations. She currently is a member of the editorial board of *Elementary School Guidance and Counseling* and represents the American School Counselor Association on the CACREP Board. She has been a school counselor and a teacher of special education.

Burl E. Gilliland is Professor and Coordinator of the Ph.D. Program in Counseling Psychology at the University of Memphis. He has had vast experience as an educator, psychologist, naval officer, law enforcement consultant, and author. In recent years he has co-authored books on crisis intervention and theories of counseling and psychotherapy. For many years Dr. Gilliland has done consultation on human relations, communication skills, group dynamics, healthcare, and other human resource areas in schools, community agencies, hospitals, police departments, higher education institutions, and mental health clinics. Since 1987 he has served as a major consultant and trainer with the Memphis Police Department in the development and implementation of the Crisis Intervention Team and the Family Trouble Center.

Larry Golden, Ph.D., is Associate Professor and Coordinator of the Counseling and Guidance Program at the University of Texas at San Antonio. He is a licensed psychologist and maintains a private practice with children and families. Dr. Golden's most recent book is *Case Studies in Child Counseling* (Macmillan, 1993). Other books are *Psychotherapeutic Techniques in School Psychology, Helping Families Help Children: Family Interventions with School Related Problems, Preventing Adolescent Suicide*, and *The Ethical Standards Casebook* (fourth edition).

Lynn Hayes is a graduate of Western Carolina University's Community Counseling Program. Ms. Hayes works as a counselor and administrator at the AIDS service organization in Asheville, North Carolina. She has worked in the field of AIDS for the past several years as a counselor, case manager, supervisor and case management administrator. As part of her work, she trains and supervises case managers and counselors in the specific area of AIDS and its unique implications. In addition to her work at the local level, she is involved at the state level in drafting and implementing HIV/AIDS case management practice standards. Lynn finds her work in the field of AIDS tremendously challenging and yet satisfying on many different levels. "Working with a client from the moment of diagnosis until the moment he/she dies has enabled me to witness and learn about some of our most difficult emotions and experiences in life. The work is often frustrating and sad but I find it hard to imagine any field as personally rewarding."

Glenda E. Isenhour, Ph.D., is the Director of Student Development at the University of Montevallo, Montevallo, Alabama. She also maintains a private practice. During the past ten years, she has presented at national, regional, and state professional counselor conferences and has conducted numerous in-service training programs in both mental health and school settings. She is the 1995-96 President for the American Mental Health Counselors Assocation.

Richard K. James, Ph. D. is a national board certified counselor and a licensed professional counselor in Tennessee. He is Professor of Counseling at the University of Memphis. He has worked closely with police departments around the country in developing crisis intervention strategies for the mentally ill and domestic violence. He has done consulting work with a variety of organizations that range from financial institutions to prison systems. Dr. James has co-authored books on theories of counseling and psychotherapy and crisis intervention as well as numerous articles and book chapters. He has been the recipient of numerous awards for his work with the mentally ill.

Frances E. Tack is a graduate student in Community Counseling at Western Carolina University. She is a graduate research assistant in that program and is currently participating in research on the consultation process. Frankie holds a bachelor's degree in industrial engineering from North Carolina State University and, after working in the business world for eight years, she recently initiated a career change from the field of engineering to counseling. She believes counseling provides a much better fit for her personality and life goals. Though she has not yet crystallized a specific field of counseling interest, Frankie is exploring working with children or college students as possible specializations.

If you are interested in contributing a case study to a subsequent edition of this text, please contact me, A. Michael Dougherty, c/o Brooks/Cole Publishing Company, 511 Forest Lodge Road, Pacific Grove, CA 93950-5098.

TO THE OWNER OF THIS BOOK:

We hope that you have found *Case Studies in Human Services Consultation* useful. So that this book can be improved in a future edition, would you take the time to complete this sheet and return it? Thank you.

School and address: _____

Department: _____

Instructor's name: _____

1. What I like most about this book is: _____

_____

2. What I like least about this book is: _____

_____

3. My general reaction to this book is: _____

_____

4. The name of the course in which I used this book is: _____

_____

5. Were all of the chapters of the book assigned for you to read? _____

   If not, which ones weren't? _____

6. In the space below, or on a separate sheet of paper, please write specific suggestions for improving this book and anything else you'd care to share about your experience in using the book.

_____

_____

_____

_____

_____

Brooks/Cole Publishing is dedicated to publishing quality books for the helping professions. If you would like to learn more about our publications, please use this mailer to request our catalogue.

Name: _____

Street Address: _____

City, State, and Zip: _____

FOLD HERE

FOLD HERE